THE PEN TURNER'S BIBLE

The Pen Turner's Bible

The Art of Creating Custom Pens

Richard Kleinhenz

LINDEN PUBLISHING

Fresno

The Pen Turner's Bible
The Art of Creating Custom Pens

by Richard Kleinhenz

Cover design: James Goold
Design and layout: Maura J. Zimmer
Photography by Richard Kleinhenz except where noted.
Drawings ©Linden Publishing Inc.

ISBN 13: 978-0-941936-61-3

Printed in China

135798642

Linden Publishing titles may be purchased in quantity at special discounts for educational, business, or promotional use. To inquire about discount pricing, please refer to the contact information below. For permission to use any portion of this book for academic purposes, please contact the Copyright Clearance Center at www.copyright.com.

Woodworking is inherently dangerous. Your safety is your responsibility.
Neither Linden Publishing nor the author assume any responsibility for any injuries or accidents.

Library of Congress Cataloging-in-Publication Data

Kleinhenz, Richard.
  The pen turner's bible : the art of creating custom pens / Richard Kleinhenz.
     p. cm.
  Includes index.
   ISBN 978-0-941936-61-3 (pbk.)
  1. Turning (Lathe work) 2. Pens. I. Title.
  TT201.K59 2012
  684'.083--dc23
              2011038622

Linden Publishing Inc.
2006 S. Mary
Fresno, CA 93721
www.lindenpub.com
800-345-4447

Table of Contents

Introduction

I turn pens for enjoyment! Having been a hobby woodworker all of my life I discovered pen making in the mid nineties and never looked back. Making pens is my passion. Many wood turners consider pens an introductory project, a learning experience on their way to bigger and better things, but there are those that get absorbed in pens—and I am one of them. I have also become involved with some Internet groups and have managed a group on Yahoo! for many years. I was a cofounder of the Penmakers' Guild, another Yahoo! group that has attracted some of the finest pen makers I know. In recent years, we have made great strides to get pens recognized as more than a beginner's project in woodturning craft circles.

Although I sell my pens through various venues, keeping my own cost low is not a primary consideration. I am not doing mass production, but working efficiently and with minimal waste of time and material is still important to me. I enjoy making some of my own tools and jigs, many of which are shared in this book.

Part of the appeal of pen making on a lathe is that a pen can be completed in one night. Even in this age of electronic communication, most of us still can't quite live without a non-electronic writing instrument, and a unique handcrafted pen adds pleasure to the use of such an old-fashioned device. As such, pens make wonderful gifts, and the craft of pen making in the home shop has grown by leaps and bounds in recent years. This in turn has taken the available hardware kits and components to levels we could only dream of in the 90s! A lot has happened since I first got involved with the craft: new styles, new materials, components with better plating, new techniques. In this book we use the latest pen kits, techniques and equipment and take the reader well past the basic kit into free design using a few purchased components. The book will introduce the reader to all of the basic techniques of making a pen on a wood lathe, with basic equipment. Some unique tools and jigs that rival or surpass commercially available tools are shown throughout the book. The first project covered in detail will get the reader to a completed modern pen that is more impressive than the slimline pen many people new to the craft tend to start out with, since those kits are most heavily marketed to the beginner. More advanced tools and techniques are introduced through over 20 pen projects, taking the reader all the way to advanced designs that make only minimal use of purchased components.

A chapter on common problems and their solutions is also included.

Inexpensive, imported metal lathes are available and open up a tremendous new area into which the pen maker can grow. We will use such a lathe not only to make our own tooling, but also to show the use of a metal lathe for most normal pen making operations. We'll discuss design considerations for a kit-less pen made from resin and go though the construction step by step.

Finally, we'll feature work by some very talented pen makers, to stimulate more creative thoughts.

Section I:
The Basics

1. Basic Tools

The lathe

Shortly after we moved into our first (and current) house in 1983 I bought a Shopsmith Mark V. The tool paid for itself very quickly. I made some furniture and the display cases for eyeglasses my wife uses in her practice. Although I used all of the multi-purpose tools, I used the lathe least of all. I made a couple of children's toys, but did not take a great liking to the lathe. In the mid 90s, at a woodworking show, I saw a gentleman from Penn State Industries turn pens. I was very taken with the result, but he used a tiny lathe, and I had a fairly large lathe at home. After watching for a while, we started talking, and when I told him I had a Shopsmith he said of course that lathe was suitable—in fact they made a special mandrel for that very lathe! I walked away from their booth with a 'starter kit' for the Shopsmith, went home and tried it. Indeed it worked! I used the Shopsmith for quite a few years as I advanced in the craft. Later I found that this starter package might not have been the best way to spend my money, but it got me going in a short time and I did not have to research the details of what I needed. The Internet was not as full of information back then as it is today! The main point is you can make pens on a large lathe, you don't *need* a mini-lathe.

Still, a mini-lathe is what I would recommend, if you don't already have a lathe in the family, or if you have a lathe along with a spouse who is unwilling to share it! A mini-lathe spins up faster, stops faster, and is often capable of higher speeds, which is an advantage for small-diameter turnings. For the same surface velocity, a small turning needs to turn much faster. You may make the final cuts on a small 6" bowl at 1000 RPM. To get the same surface speed on a ½" diameter pen the lathe would have to turn at 12000 RPM! There are some practical limits. Large lathes usually go up to 2000 or 2500 RPM, mini-lathes tend

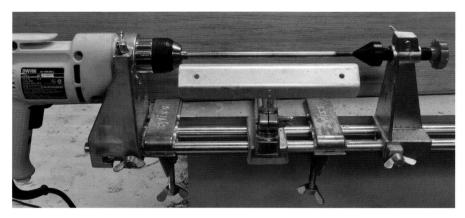

1. Drill-driven jigs can be used but it is difficult to produce a good pen on one of these.

2. This pen was made on the lathe shown above. It was a challenge!

to go to 4000-5000 RPM. The main point is that spindle speed and turning diameter are related, and lathes are optimized for what they need to do. A suitable brand-new mini-lathe can often be had in the $200–300 range.

What distinguishes mini-lathes and makes one lathe more desirable than another? Other than brand, reputation, warranty and the likes you should look for a spindle with a Morse-taper 2 (MT2). It just makes life simpler, since accessories are more widely available than for the smaller MT1. A MT2 has more holding power than an MT1, which might be an issue if you try to use a large drill bit on the lathe.

You can get all the tooling you need for a smaller lathe with MT1 also, you'll just have fewer choices. Several lathes with MT1 spindles are marketed as pen lathes. In general, I would recommend against a lathe smaller than the MT1 spindle lathe. You can use contraptions that are driven by a portable drill. Grizzly sells such an item for under $50, or you can get an accessory to the Swiss-made Zyliss vise (see Photo 1). I also remember a young man that made his own mount for a drill and made pens on that until he made enough money to afford a better lathe. You can definitely make pens on such a device (Photo 2), but in general it is much more difficult for a novice turner to achieve acceptable results.

So look for MT2 in headstock and tailstock. In the US a 1" x 8TPI is a desirable thread on the spindle nose, again because it is the most common on this size lathe and accessories are the easiest to find. The other basic decision is variable speed or not. Most lathes have a belt-drive system; even in variable speed (VS) lathes there generally are several belt positions available. Ultimately it is a question of cost—VS lathes cost a little more, but today there are quite a few VS mini-lathes on the market and competition has reduced the price for VS. A minor brand VS speed lathe is often the same as a name brand multi-speed. The Shopsmith I started with had variable speed, and I did not get a mini-lathe until the Nova Mercury came to the US market. I think it was the first affordable mini-lathe with VS. Today every brand seems to have a VS offering. I highly recommend getting VS, but it is not absolutely necessary. You can work with a multi-speed lathe, either by getting used to frequent belt changes (in which case make sure you get a model that facilitates that with ease) or by adapting your techniques such that you don't have to change speeds too often.

On a VS lathe look for the widest control range within a given belt setting. Some lathes cover a factor of more than 13x on a given belt setting, others only 2.4x on each setting and less than 10x overall. A wide range is very advantageous for pen turning. I think manufacturers limit the controllers at the low end because there is relatively little torque available in these DC motors at low speed. For large turnings, the low speed is needed to rough uneven pieces, so you do need high torque at low speeds. For pens, we don't need torque. I never turn at the low speed settings, but it is very convenient for applying finish. I use cyanoacrylate (CA) glue and I am quite happy that it is not flung out from a fast turning blank!

Some of the newer lathes feature electronic speed readout. I consider that a gimmick. I generally adjust speed by feel and not by some number. In fact when someone asks me at what speed I do a certain operation, I need to do that operation, setting the speed by feel, and then look on the dial.

One other option to consider is a metal lathe. A small metal lathe can cost about the same as a mini-wood lathe! For certain operations the wood lathe is more suited, but you *can* turn wood on a metal lathe, using normal wood chisels, and also do a lot of operations not so easily done on a wood lathe. We'll cover the metal lathe and its unique capabilities in a later chapter.

Lathe tools

There is a myriad of turning tools on the market to do any number of specialized operations. I would recommend a single tool to start with, a ½" spindle gouge made of a good quality steel. Carbon steel tools, the least expensive, are becoming difficult to find. Almost everything available these days is high-speed steel (HSS) of one sort or another. HSS holds an edge longer than carbon steel, which means less honing and sharpening. It is also more heat tolerant than carbon steel and thus easier to sharpen without losing the temper. This tool is also referred to as a 'shallow gouge' or a 'detail gouge'. Often it is a ½" round bar with a shallow groove cut into the top. A bowl gouge will have a deep groove, and it makes it harder to see what is going on at the cut. Most spindle gouges come ground to a 30° angle at the tip with very little side-cut. I reground mine to a 'fingernail profile' that many bowl turners like. I ground it at a 45° angle. My rationale when I first did this was that the steeper angle will have a stronger edge and will need less frequent sharpening. I have no data to back up this theory but continue to be happy with the grind.

The second tool you should get is a thin parting tool. It is needed for some types of pens. A regular ³⁄₁₆" parting tool can also be used in most cases.

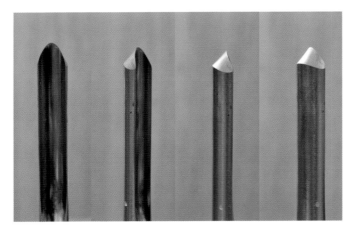

3. This is the grind I use on my spindle gouge. It is about 45 degrees, steeper than a factory grind of 30 degrees.

Making a Thin Parting Tool

You can use a piece of a worn out band saw blade to make a thin parting tool. Ask in a machine shop to have the next blade they are replacing saved for you! I used a piece of ¾" blade I discarded from my wood band saw. Use a Dremel tool with a cutoff disk to cut about an 8 or 10" section of the blade. Cut one end at about a 30° angle, with the long point on the side with the teeth. Grind the teeth off making sure you don't overheat the blade and lose the temper. The area next to the teeth is generally hard; the body is often softer steel. Make some sort of handle for it and sharpen it by adding a small backgrind at the point. The cuts we are making are small and this tool has worked very nicely for me!

A homemade, thin, parting tool made from a discarded saw blade.

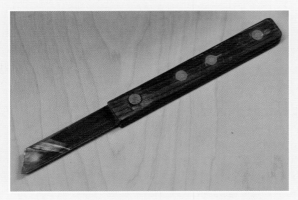

I consider a skew optional. Some people will only work with the skew, and I actually also use it a lot, but that comes down to personal preference. The ½" spindle gouge is more forgiving, and by using a swept back fingernail grind as I showed in Photo 3 you can make a cut very much like the planing cut of a skew. Scrapers, roughing gouges, you can use any of these, but you sure don't need them.

The next tool is an absolute necessity, a sharpening system. A 3450 RPM 8" grinder and a good jig is the least expensive way to go. A slower speed 1725 RPM grinder is an option but not necessary. (These RPMs are standard for induction motors in the US. Other parts of the world with 50 Hz AC will have slightly different speeds). Usually these slow speed grinders cost a little more since they are less common. The slow speed is more forgiving if you use carbon steel tools since less heat is produced. A good set of blue aluminum oxide wheels with 80 and 120 grits can be bought at places like Woodcraft or Rockler and is a good investment. White aluminum oxide wheels in the same grits cost less and work OK. All the woodworking catalogs and websites have recommendations, and the limiter will be your budget. The standard gray wheels that probably came with the $39.99 grinder are not suitable; they are meant for softer steels.

There are lots of jigs on the market to hold your tools and give a consistent grind. They all work well once you have them set up and adjusted to produce the grind you like. You can even find plans on the Internet to make your own jig if you're so inclined. I use a Tormek slow-speed wet grinder with jigs and have never regretted the investment. The only bad thing about it is its cost. Today several knock-offs are on the market and even Tormek is now offering a smaller version that takes most of the same highly evolved jigs as the large T-7. The small T-3 version is perfect for turning tools!

Most turning tools you buy are not ready to use. You need to sharpen and hone them! The carbide-tools that have become available in recent years are an exception. Most of these have a replaceable insert. I am not particularly expert with these, for me they fix a problem I don't have! But a novice turner

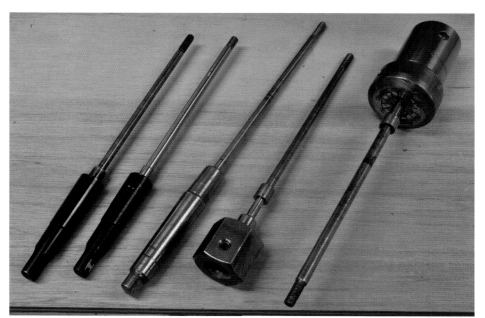

4. Pen mandrels, from left: "A" precision mandrel, "B" precision mandrel, standard pen mandrel in Morse-taper two, a specific mandrel for use on the Shopsmith, my usual setup, a mandrel-rod in a Beall collet chuck.

Mandrel Sizes

There are two common mandrel sizes on the market. The 'A' size is the most common. There are small differences between suppliers, so it is best to pick the supplier where you will be buying your pen kits and use their mandrel. Penn State Industries uses a mandrel with a diameter of .245", Berea's mandrel is .246". That small difference is enough to make for some incompatibility that can frustrate the novice pen maker. The second mandrel size is the 'B' mandrel, and it is .290" diameter. It is only used by Berea and the retailers they supply. A 'B' mandrel is 40% stronger than an 'A' mandrel. The 'A' mandrel is sometimes referred to as the 7 mm mandrel. The 'B' mandrel is an 8 mm mandrel. These names come from the outer diameter of the brass tubes that slip onto them.

mightconsider such a tool. The cutting tip is very hard, and once it no longer cuts like new you can just rotate it slightly and bring a new cutting edge forward. Once a tip is used up you replace it with a new insert.

Tools for pen making

There are very few specialized tools you need to make pens. A pen mandrel is used to hold the pen barrel for turning and finishing. There are ways to turn without a pen mandrel. For example, closed end pens as shown in Chapter 18 use a completely different kind of mandrel. Most people however, start out with a regular pen mandrel. The mandrel is typically fitted in a Morse taper which has to match your headstock. Photo 4 shows some mandrel systems. Some mandrels are adjustable in length—a desirable feature. If you have a metal lathe it is easy to make a mandrel. I will show you in Chapter 29.

The tailstock end of the mandrel needs to be supported, most conveniently via a revolving center mounted in the tailstock ram. This is often referred to as a live center, and while technically this expression is incorrect according to experts who never seem to get tired of stressing that point, this is what we will call it here since everyone I know calls it that! Many lathes come with a live center as shown in Photo 5 on the left. Notice the sharp center prong. This type of center is *not* suitable to support a mandrel! The type that is needed is shown on the right and is called a 60° center because of the angle of the prong. It is very common in metal machining and can be bought quite inexpensively; see Resources on page 141. If you look closely at the end of the mandrel, you will see a drilled center hole and a conical countersunk surface. That surface is 60° and needs to match the live center. A sharp center will usually bottom out in the hole, the prong will wear, the mandrel will not run true and it will be the source of much frustration. Get a 60° live center!

The last specialized tool you should have is a pen mill, a.k.a. barrel trimmer. These come in different diameters, a ⅝" size is the best place to start (Photo 6). Later on you will most likely add a larger trimmer also. You may be tempted to have one tool do all (I know I did when I started, but I didn't have this book to tell me better!), but because large diameter trimmers have to cut more wood, they require more effort, and also are more prone to tearing off chunks of material any time the blank that is being cut is smaller than the diameter of the trimmer. I have never felt the need to buy one of the barrel trimmer systems with many pilot shafts. I think you will always be missing a size for the next kit that comes out, and changing pilots is cumbersome. I would recommend getting the simple 7 mm trimmer, and in Chapter 4 I will show you how to adapt it to any pen kit.

This covers the essential tools for an initial shopping list. There are some specific tools and jigs needed for each pen kit, some of which I will show you how to make yourself. I will mention a few more optional tools that are great to have around.

5. Live centers: From the left: A center with a sharp point that comes standard with many lathes. This type is not usable for pen turning; a 60-degree live center; the compact 60-degree live center I use on my pen lathes wastes less space than the larger center in the middle.

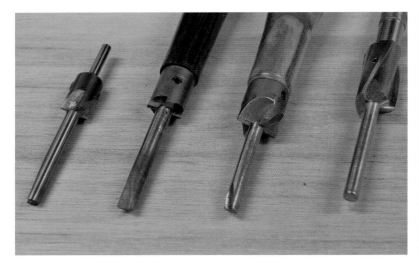

6. Various pen mills. From the left: a pen mill for use in a drill; a pen mill with a larger shaft for larger diameter brass tubes in a homemade handle; a pen mill with a standard shaft in a homemade handle, and a counterbore with a replaceable pilot adapted for pens.

Tip: **Replacement Mandrels**
Mandrel rods can usually be replaced when they get bent without replacing the Morse taper. Look for a system where this is possible. In particular, adjustable mandrels have replaceable rods so a larger initial investment is quickly recovered.

2. Drilling

Even experienced woodturners find drilling pen blanks frustrating, but with the right equipment and some care, drilling should not be a challenge. We'll look at all aspects of this operation in some detail.

Equipment

Strictly speaking, it is not necessary to use a drill press, but it is the tool specifically developed and optimized for drilling and thus most people will tend to use it, especially if they already *have* a suitable drill press. Alternatives to the drill press would be drilling on the lathe, or using a hand held power drill and drill guide. Penn State Industries sells such a jig, it involves hardened bushings and a guide onto which a pen blank is clamped. This type of drill jig is only available in a few sizes, severely limiting the types of pens you can make. I'd stay away from it and use a lathe instead.

A lathe can be used in two ways. You can mount a Jacobs chuck in the spindle, and use a sled on the bed to advance a pen blank clamped onto it into the spinning drill bit. Such an arrangement is sold by HUT for the Sherline lathe. With a clever lever operated feed arrangement this sounds like a good solution available to Sherline users. Not owning a Sherline I have never used it. Of course it is possible to build such a sled for any other lathe. More commonly, people drill on the lathe by chucking up the blank in a four-jaw chuck, and using a stationary drill bit in a Jacobs chuck mounted in the tailstock. This arrangement works well as long as the tailstock and

1. Drilling on the lathe using a four jaw chuck and a drill chuck in the tailstock.

2. A rotating collar depth stop allows you to set the drill depth so you can avoid having the drill bit exit the blank.

3. A rod-type depth stop has some advantages.

spindle are well aligned. If not, instead of a straight hole you get a tapered hole that can be problematic. Since you probably need to retract the bit a few times to clear out chips, and since the feed speed of the tailstock ram is usually slow, this technique works but is a little slow. A drill press is the ideal tool for drilling pen blanks.

If you are buying a drill press, there are some things to look for that will improve its usability for pen blank drilling. Since for some pen models fairly long holes need to be drilled, a long 'stroke' is highly desirable. The stroke is the maximum distance the drill chuck can travel vertically. Try to get at least 3¼"—this will let you do most pen blanks without having to reposition the blank. Longer is better, some drill presses offer 5" and more.

There are two sorts of depth stops commonly used in drill presses. One type is a rotating collar (Photo 2). Another is a straight rod with an adjustable nut that limits the depth (Photo 3). I prefer the latter. The reasons are explained below in the section on drilling blind holes for closed end pens

Most drill presses will have a table that can be raised or lowered, and clamped on the column. A rack and pinion arrangement is nice, allowing easier fine adjustment. Usually the table can also be tilted. It is important that the tilt can be locked securely, something to check if you purchase a used drill press.

Drill bits

There is quite a variety of bits, and they do not all perform the same. The most common bit is the twist bit. (A in Photo 4) I have a set of inexpensive drill bits, 115 bits total, which includes letter and number sizes, as well as fraction sizes in ¹⁄₆₄" increments up to ½". Such a set can be bought for $30–$40 on sale

from places like Enco or Harbor Freight. They are not terribly high quality, and although they are made from high-speed steel (HSS) the steel is usually not very good so they may dull fairly quickly if used in a professional environment. They are meant to be used in metal, and will last a long time in wood. If sharpened properly they can perform quite well. The advantage of such a set is that you are almost guaranteed to find a suitable bit for any pen drilling operation under ½" in the set. Usually these bits do not come to a point, but rather a chisel edge at the point so when they enter the wood they will try to find their own entry point. You can help that by giving the bit an entry point where you want, using a center punch.

There are high-end versions of these twist drill bits available also. They tend to be somewhat pricey. The difference is that they are usually made in the US from a tougher alloy, and will stay sharp much longer. I have a few of these bits, made by Norseman, and they perform quite well.

A close cousin of the twist drill bit is the parabolic bit (B in Photo 4). Its flutes have a different shape, and they cut very aggressively. I find that parabolic bits are too grabby in many woods for my liking. It feels like they want to pull the bit into the wood, and you have to have a steady hand at the drill press quill.

A bradpoint bit (C in Photo 4) is a bit specifically designed for wood. It has a center spur that makes it easier to enter at a specific point, and is supposed to help it drill straight. The cutting edge is flat or rounded, depending on the manufacturer, but in all cases there is a cutting spur at the perimeter that defines the hole diameter. I have tried bradpoint bits, and was not too happy with them. I think the design is for drilling into face grain, not into end grain as we usually do for pens. In end grain, I found they were not very good at drilling straight. I think this is because the center spur actually cuts with the sides, not the point, and that edge of the center spur is easily pushed aside by grain that's

4. Drill bits, from the left: jobber bit, parabolic bit, bradpoint bit, and pilot-point bit.

running at a slight angle to it. I have tried inexpensive Chinese bradpoint bits as well as high-end Swiss-made ones with similar results.

The bit I use whenever I can is the pilot-point bit (D in Photo 4). It is often referred to as 'bullet bit', which is what it was first marketed as by Black and Decker some years ago. The bit has a flat cutting face, with a short protruding bit that's ground like a centering drill. I find of all the bits it cuts the straightest. These bits are currently marketed in the US by DeWalt, and are sometimes available locally in some of the major home improvement centers. They are not inexpensive, but I find they are worth it because they are better at cutting straight than any other bit I've tried. You can find 29-piece sets up to ½" in 64th inch increments on eBay for under $40 at times. One disadvantage of these bits is that they are not so easily sharpened.

Sizes over ½" are a special challenge; you can't find pilot point bits over ½" (other than 13 mm bits available in Europe). Many standard drill chucks only have a grip capacity of ½". Large bits with a shank that is turned down to ½" or even ⅜" are known as Silver and Deming and are available in any diameter interesting to pen turners, in 64th inch increments, as well as metric sizes. US-made high-end bits are available in these large sizes also, and I have had excellent results with these. You can also get an inexpensive Chinese bit and sharpen it using a device sold as 'Drill Doctor'.

This is not an exhaustive listing of drill bit types, there are certainly more, but these are the types most frequently sold through pen turning supply catalogs, and of most interest to pen turners.

Drilling Jigs

To drill a pen blank, it must be held such that the drill bit enters in the top center and drills straight down the middle. There are lots of ways to achieve this! You can make your own jig, or buy a commercial one. I started drilling on my Shopsmith using a home made jig that performed very well. Photo 5 is fairly self-explanatory, the jig clamps to the table, and adjustment for blank size is accomplished by raising or lowering the table slightly.

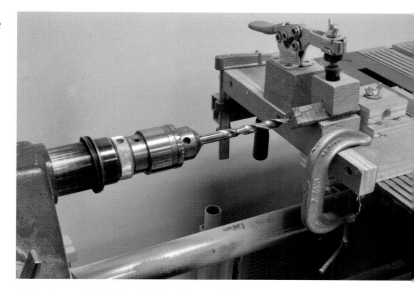

5. A shopmade drilling jig for a Shopsmith.

Improve Performance on Inexpensive Drill Bits

High quality bits are available in large sizes, but start getting very costly. A ³⁷/₆₄" Norseman drill bit as required for some of the larger kits will set you back nearly $30. I have one of these and really like it, but you can also get an inexpensive Chinese bit and sharpen it using a device sold as 'Drill Doctor'. The Drill Doctor is not expensive and is a slightly simplified plastic version of a commercial drill-sharpening jig. You may be able to find one on sale for a little over $100. Make sure you get the model that accepts bits larger than ½"! I have had very good luck with these on the large bits. I find a cheap Chinese bit sharpened to 135 degrees split point with the Drill Doctor will cut as well as a high-end bit.

An inexpensive drill bit (right) can be ground on a Drill Doctor with a split point to drill like a high-end bit.

6. This simple drill jig is no longer commercially made but it is easy to make it yourself and it performs excellently.

7. A drill jig sold by several large pen turning suppliers.

At some point I moved to a dedicated drill press, and have used a variety of commercial jigs over the years. Since models change all the time I will use some commercial jigs to illustrate points rather than review specific jigs.

The purpose of a pen drill jig is to hold a pen blank securely and square. One extremely simple and inexpensive drill jig that meets those goals is shown in Photo 6. It's best to have a waste board on the table, not just to protect your table, but also to avoid a 'blow out' in case you drill through. To line up the jig, put a pen blank with marked center in the jig, line that center up under the bit, then clamp the far end of the drill jig to the table. You can then drill the blank, clamp the next blank and drill it. Minor adjustments to accommodate different size blanks can be made by nudging the jig around the single clamping point. I found this jig extremely effective and fast! The important thing is to make sure the Vee-cut is precise so a blank is held vertically.

Most of the commercial pen-drilling jigs are self-centering, i.e. both jaws move at the same time. Once set up and aligned, blanks of different size can be drilled without the need to re-align.

A common type of self-centering jig is sold through several stores with only slight variation (like color). (see Photo 7) It has a shortcoming in that only one side of the bracket (opposite the crank) is screwed down to the base. When you withdraw a drill bit that is clogged, as happens easily in certain oily woods like

cocobolo, the whole jig can flex up. This increases the friction and makes it hard to withdraw the bit. The hole will become oval, and the blank heats up more and may even crack. Other than that, the jig worked fairly well for me. The knob moves the jaws easily. Perhaps a little too easily; I found vibrations could easily release the clamp.

Photo 8 shows a jig sold by Penn State Industries. The point that attracted me to this jig is that both sides are screwed to the base. The jig also has excellent capacity; it allows you to hold bottle stopper blanks for drilling. Unfortunately, after I drilled two blanks, I noticed something was wrong. The whole jig felt loose. I quickly found the problem. The guide rods are screwed together, and mine rattled loose

8. A drill jig sold by Penn State Industries holds the blank securely. A newer version of this jig has a replaceable waste block which is a nice feature.

9. The Lee Valley drill jig.

immediately! Luckily, this was easy to fix, using some Loctite. After that, the jig worked well. The large crank operates the jaws very comfortably.

Another jig by Lee Valley also had a simple defect in that a guide bushing was not securely attached to the jaw. I had to fix that one also. The jig is locked down on both sides; the three guide rods seemed to be a good idea but in practical use I found the jig often got stuck, the jaws got cocked on the guide rods and needed to be freed manually.

The best jig that I know of (Photo 10) is made in limited production by Paul Huffman and available from Classic Nib (see Resources on page 141). This jig

10. The Paul Huffman drill jig is the Cadillac of drill jigs.

is simply in a class by itself. The immediate difference from the commercial jigs is that the two guide rods that guide the jaws are off to one side, and arranged vertically. The obvious advantage is that the jig can be loaded and unloaded with ease. Because of the open design it offers the same loading/unloading ease as the simple wooden jig, and is much faster than any of the other self-centering jigs! The guide rods are supported on both sides, thus there is no jaw lifting issue. The capacity is the largest of any out there; 3" diagonal. What I particularly like is the fact that the jaws are raised from the mounting platform. This allows a waste board to be inserted under the blank, and the jaws move above it. I used some scrap plywood and cut it into strips that just fit between the stationary brackets. This is the costliest of the jigs, but it's the Cadillac amongst these jigs, and will give excellent service for many years.

Setting up the drill press

To drill accurately, you have to make sure the path the drill bit follows goes straight down the middle of the blank. So you must make sure that the table is square to the bit. My drill press has two aligned holes and a pin that supposedly aligns the table perpendicular to the bit. I found it does not in mine, so don't rely on that! To make sure the table is square, I chuck a piece of straight steel rod in my drill chuck. A 'drill blank' is great for that. It is ground precisely and is very straight. A second blank is then clamped in the drilling jig. The two blanks are brought next to each other. It is very easy to judge if they run parallel. If you see a widening gap loosen the table tilt nut (under the table) and make an adjustment. Retighten and look again. You can also check front to back by lining up the two rods the other way. But there is generally no adjustment there. If you find the table is tilted fore or aft, you have to work something with shims or get a better drill press.

Once the table is square it is very easy to set up the self-centering vise. Remove the rod from the drill vise. Lower the chuck so that the drill rod goes into the jig, lock the quill, and clamp the jig to the rod. Now clamp the jig to the table. Release the jig jaws, and remove the rod. Your jig is aligned perfectly to the chuck and you can keep drilling blanks of all sizes and use all sorts of drill bits until you drill something like antler when you may have to choose a drill path that does *not* go down the center.

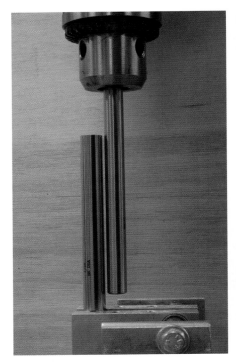 

11. Squaring the table using 2 steel rods.   **12.** My drill jig, using a X-Y vise and a Paul Huffman jig.

My own arrangement looks a little bit like a Rube Goldberg contraption, but it performs marvelously. (see Photo 12). Instead of clamping the drill jig to the table, I mounted an X-Y vise on the drill press, and it then holds the drilling jig. This gives me the repeatability of the drill jig, yet lets me move off center in a controlled way for antler drilling.

Drilling techniques

Most drill presses are multi-speed. Choosing the right drill speed is important. As you drill, you generate heat which is a bad thing and should be avoided! In plastic materials, heat will lead to melting. The result is a distressed drill bit and generally a ruined blank. The heat is generated by the front cutting edges slicing through the material. The chips that are generated by that slicing action are transported up the flutes of the drill bit which acts as an Archimedes screw. However, chips are not always removed efficiently. Some tend to become stuck partway up and pack into the flutes of the bit. As soon as that happens, more heat is generated by those plugs rubbing on the sides of the hole. Retract the drill often, and clear the flutes. Certain woods are notorious for packing in the flutes. Cocobolo and desert ironwood come to mind. In some woods you can see a whitish circle appearing briefly as you drill. That is steam generated by evaporating moisture in the wood. This situation should be avoided! Obviously a dull drill bit will rub more, instead of slicing, and generate more heat. It is very important to use sharp bits!

I generally drill wood around 2000 RPM. The fast speed allows a faster feed rate, thus less time to generate heat. Some people swear by drilling with the slowest speed, around 500 RPM for many drill presses. I find no advantage in that. I am not religious about the drill speed in wood, anything over 1200 works just fine, for any size drill.

For plastics, I drill around 700–1000 RPM, a value found by experience. You have to watch the chips, or rather ribbons coming up the flutes. If the waste starts looking soft, stop! You're a step away from melting the plastic.

> *Tip:* Sometimes it is not possible to leave the extra ¼" that allows drilling short. The best thing is to glue a short waste block to the blank.

There are two types of problems commonly encountered in drilling. One is not drilling straight. The drill bit may enter in the center of the blank, but the other end is not centered, or the bit even emerges at the side. If the jig is squared to the drill axis, and you use a sharp pilot-point bit this problem is easily avoided. Using a larger blank of course also helps, giving more margin for error, but 'jumbo' sized pen blanks add cost. The other common problem is referred to as blowout. The blank just splits or a large section breaks away. Sometimes this is due to a dull bit or too high a feed rate. Most of the time a blowout happens when the drill bit exits the wood. At the point, the slicing edges of the drill bit try to slice through fibers that are not supported, and will easily catch and break off a section. It is the same effect as when a block plane slicing end grain goes off the end of the board. If the fibers are not supported, they will tend to tear out. This can be helped by having a waste board under the drill blank, but I find this method only partially effective. The best prevention is to avoid the situation! Cut your blank ¼" longer than required! Use the depth stop of the drill press to limit the travel so that the drill bit will not exit the blank. After drilling saw the blank to the proper length. The saw cut will intersect the drilled hole and open up the end of the blank. With this method blowouts will be all but totally eliminated!

Sometimes, when a blowout happens despite the best prevention, maybe on a piece of burl that had a weak spot already, you can use superglue and re-attach the piece seamlessly. Then carefully finish the drilling, using a very low feed rate. The repair can be nearly invisible.

Note: Cardinal rule for drilling pen blanks: Cut long, drill short, then cut to proper length!

If you have a drill press with a short stroke, like 2", you can still use it to drill longer blanks. Do not try to drill from two sides and expect the holes to meet up in the middle! The best method is to drill as deep as the drill press allows. Then raise the drill bit partially and lock the quill. Unclamp the drill jig, put a piece of wood of suitable thickness (say ¾") under the jig, and lock it in place again. The drill bit that is still in the partially drilled hole assures alignment. Now you can drill that extra ¾". Raising the table does not work so well, because most drill columns are round, and will not go up straight forcing a re-alignment anyway. Also, raising and reclamping the blank in the vise is not ideal because often blanks are not straight and reclamping changes the axis.

Tip: Sometimes you find yourself pulling out a kit for which you don't find the instructions. Or the instructions call for a drill bit you don't have—say a metric bit. This is where a drill chart comes in handy! One of the kit distributors, HUT Products, has a very convenient drill chart posted on their website. I have copied and laminated it, and it is always handy in my shop. The chart lists metric, fraction, and letter size bits and gives their decimal equivalent. You can simply use calipers to measure a brass tube, find the size in the chart, and choose a slightly larger drill bit that you have. With a 115 bit drill set that includes number, letter and fractional sizes you can always find a suitable drill bit (up to ½")! You generally don't want to drill the exact size you measured, usually this will result in a hole that's a little tight. The size of the hole you drill in wood depends on a lot of parameters, from the type of wood, your drill press, and the drilling parameters like feed rate and speed. Pen kit suppliers know this and generally advise a drill size that is slightly large. Sometimes their recommendation will not work for you! Since you also want to leave a little room for glue, the starting size to choose should be .005"–.010" larger than the measured brass tube diameter. After a few trials you will find what works best for you.

3. Materials

There is a wide variety of materials available to the pen maker. In this chapter I will show you a variety, and that's really just scratching the surface! Of course there is wood. Straight grain wood is easy to find and to make into a pen. In the beginning, you should look for hard woods; softwoods add a little challenge. Look for woods with tight grain structure so you can see some color variation on the small barrel that makes up a pen. You can add a little variety by obtaining pen blanks cut at an angle, or cutting wood at an angle if you make your own. Wood should be dry. If it is not, the pen will crack. Wood shrinks as it dries; the brass tube we will glue into it prevents it from shrinking so it will crack!

An interesting variation is burl wood.

The grain is wild and thus the turning is a tad more challenging. Many burl woods are available from pen blank suppliers. Other interesting variations include spalted wood and special grain formations like birdseye or curly maple.

Dymond wood is a lamination of thin layers of dyed woods impregnated with a resin. It is very dense and a little tougher to cut than wood. Available in many colors, it makes interesting pens when you are looking for specific colors, for example to match school or team colors.

Angle-cut tulip wood.

A fine burl.

Dymond wood.

Curly or fiddle-back grain in koa.

You can cut aluminum with woodworking tools! You can get barrels that are already drilled or you can buy stock and do it yourself!

There are several stone products on the market that lend themselves to making pens. These manmade stones are marketed under a variety of names like Tru-stone or Gemstone. They are very hard but workable with standard woodturning tools. Note that not all varieties are the same hardness!

Solid surface materials are easy to find from countertop suppliers. They typically discard sink cutouts which you can cut up yourself. Or you can find pen blanks from Corian and similar materials on eBay.

Aluminum.

Tru-stone.

Corian.

Drying Wood Using a Microwave Oven

If you harvest some wood locally, say from storm damage or pruning, it is green. You can cut it into oversize pen blanks on a band saw, approximately 1" x 1" x 6". Dry them for about a year. To accelerate the drying, you can use your microwave oven! Weigh the blanks on an accurate scale and record the weight. Put them in the microwave on defrost for two minutes covered by a paper towel. Wait until they are *completely* cooled off. Reweigh them and subtract the new weight from the weight before the cycle to get the amount of weight lost. Wait until the wood has cooled off completely, then repeat this cycle until you don't see the weight change anymore. Microwave ovens vary, so time and power are not absolutes. Stay close when you have them in the microwave and check a few times in the middle of the first cycle. You don't want to set them on fire!

There is a *huge* variety of resin pen blanks available. The offerings change over time. You can find old resins that are rather heat sensitive, or new ones that are often more tolerant, in colors that match any mood you may be in!

Deer antler is another material that offers a unique challenge but makes beautiful pens in several looks, depending on the antler species and the way it is cut. Antler is discarded annually, so no animal has to die for the antler. Hunters are often a good source for antler pieces sufficiently big to make pens from. The easiest way to obtain antler suitable for pens is from the companies that supply the pen makers' market; see Resources on page 141.

To add variety you can obtain laminated pen blanks. An interesting variation that you can also make yourself was available once as busy-block. Stock up on blanks you like; they may not be available in the future.

Resin.

Deer antler.

Busy-Block.

Laminated wood.

You can also laminate your own blank for any number of creative effects.

You can use clear acrylic resin to cast pen blanks, and encapsulate all sorts of things. Commercially available clear-cast blanks include snake skin and printed circuit boards. The material cuts easily and can be polished to a great shine.

Mokume gane is an ancient Japanese technique of forging contrasting metals together. In recent years a material with somewhat similar effect has become available, called Mokume M3 (macromolecular metal). It is high percentage metal with a bonding agent, cuts very easily with wood tools and can be polished with metal polishes. It is very pricey but does make a stunning pen.

Last, I want to show a corncob. You can get dried seed corn from a pet store, or buy a prepared stabilized corncob that has been dyed in a variety of colors. It makes a beautiful pen!

Segmented.

Snake skin, under cast acrylic.

Corn cob.

Mokume M3.

4. First Pen: Gatsby Ballpoint Pen

Y ou have seen this pen in many materials in the last chapter. It is a great first pen! In the past, many people (including myself) started with a slimline pen. A slimline is inexpensive and simple, but also can be difficult to get perfect! The transition from the pen barrel to the tip has to be spot on both in terms of concentricity and diameter or it is very noticeable.

There are several variations of this pen, available from different suppliers. It is not an accident that I chose the Gatsby. It is more tolerant in terms of diameter than, for example, the Sierra from Berea Hardwoods or the Sienna from Craft Supplies. Both ends of the barrel are bounded by a double bead and if you don't get the diameter perfect or have a little eccentricity in your pen this will hide it. Of course there is a single barrel only to turn which makes it a fast gratification project! You use only half a standard pen blank so you save a little in the overall cost of the pen. There are several similar single-barrel pen kits on the market, such as the Majestic Squire, the Art Deco, the Elegant Sierra, etc. I like the Gatsby/Sierra/Sienna because it shows a little more wood than some of the other pens.

We will use a stabilized Norway maple pen blank. 'Stabilized' means the wood has been dried and then gone through a process that fills

Tools & Materials

- Lathe and standard tooling
- Gatsby twist pen kit from Penn State Industries (PSI)
- Bushings for Gatsby pen (PSI)
- Pen mill shim barrel (PSI)
- Alternative for pen mill shim barrel: 7 mm brass tube (PSI) and scrap wood or Corian
- Stabilized pen blank
- $^{27}/_{64}$" drill bit

1. It helps to study the parts and lay them out according to the instructions.

all internal air spaces with a resinous substance, effectively sealing it. Ambient humidity will no longer affect the wood. It will not move with seasonal changes like 'normal' wood does. It is also very easy to give it a great shine without a lot of effort. Stabilized wood costs a little more than natural wood, but remember we can get two pens out of a single barrel, and it is easier to achieve great results with stabilized wood.

Read the instructions that came with the pen and lay all the parts out in the same arrangement as on the pen. Mark the blank to the length of the brass tube plus about ¼".

Cutting the blank

I cut blanks on my band saw. Other power saws with appropriate fences may also be used, like a table saw or chop saw, and of course, you could use a handsaw and miterbox. I use a very simple jig on my band saw, a 6" x 6" piece of scrap plywood. I press the wood against the fence and the pen blank against the jig and feed both together into the blade. After a while the jig has lots of little cuts and I just start using a different corner. There are eight positions, and when it gets too chopped up I use the next square. It's a very simple jig but highly effective. I simply set the fence position using the brass tube as a gauge, adding a ¼" or so.

2. Cutting the blank on a band saw with a simple jig. The wasteblock is used to keep the blank square.

Tip: *Some woods cannot be stabilized because they are too dense. Examples are ebony and snakewood. You may see ads for stabilized snakewood at a higher cost— don't go for it, you can put it through the process but the wood will not absorb any of the resin.*

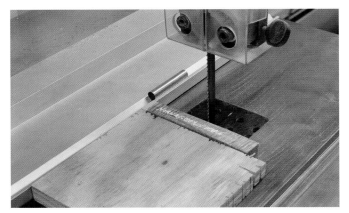

3. It helps to mark the blank center before drilling.

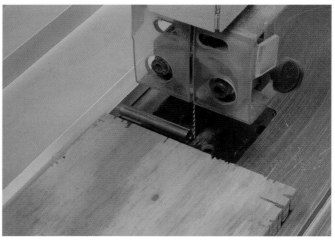

4. The brass tube is used to set the length for the second cut.

Drilling the blank

With a well-aligned jig you don't have to mark the blank, but it doesn't hurt. Draw two lines connecting opposite corners to find the center. Lock a $^{27}/_{64}$" bit in the drill chuck. Set the depth stop such that the drill bit stops just before the waste board by advancing the bit down, clamping the quill and running the depth stop to the limit. Release the quill and check that indeed the bit stops in the right place! Set the drill press to 2000 RPM or thereabouts. Drill in stages. Advance ½" and withdraw the bit, then another ½" and so on. Some materials allow more depth at a time. How far you can drill at a time is something you learn with experience.

Since our blank was ¼" longer than the brass tube and we did not drill all the way through we need to go back to the band saw. I like having my fence in the low position so I have clearance for my left hand. If your band saw does not allow that, make an auxiliary fence from a piece of wood, 5" wide. With the saw turned off, I use the brass tube as a gauge. I set the fence so that the teeth of the blade just miss the end of the brass tube. I leave no more than ¹/₃₂" gap! The

5. For a safe cut, you can use a straight piece of wood as a low secondary fence to make room for your hand on the left of the blade.

key is to have the blank to the left side of the blade, against a low fence that allows your hand to move safely. If your saw only has a tall fence suitable for resawing, you can make a quick auxiliary low fence by putting down a straight board next to the tall fence. Cutting close to the desired length avoids having to trim large amounts of wood later. Check the final length and the fit of the brass tube. It should fully disappear in the hole and have very little wood at either end. It should also slide freely.

Gluing and squaring

Before gluing in the brass tube it's a good idea to roughen it up slightly with sand paper. It removes surface films from the manufacturer, or your own handling, and provides a better surface for the glue to adhere to.

> *Tip:* With non-stabilized woods sometimes the blank moves right after you drill it and the tube will not slide in freely. This is something the wood is doing, you did nothing wrong! You can work on the hole using an 8" round bastard file until you get a nice sliding fit.

6. To avoid getting glue inside the tube use Play-Doh to plug the end of the brass tube.

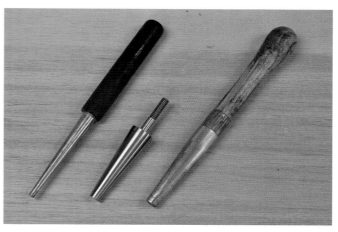

7. A common commercial insertion tool is limited to smaller brass tubes, another commercial tool suitable for larger tubes, and my homemade tool in a turned handle.

When we glue the brass tube into the blank, we want to avoid getting glue on the inside of the brass tube, which would have to be removed later. So we plug the side of the brass tube that is inserted into the hole. Play-Doh makes a very good plug, flatten some out and use the brass tube like a cookie-cutter. Dental base wax is another option that works well; it is available in thin sheets.

To glue the brass tube into the drilled blank I highly recommend using epoxy glue. So-called 5-minute epoxy is a good choice. Squeeze equal amounts of the two components (hardener and resin) onto a mixing pad and stir them together using a toothpick or Popsicle stick until they are thoroughly mixed. Spread some glue inside the drilled blank. Hold the blank on an 'insertion tool' or something similar to avoid getting glue all over your fingers. The photo shows a tool I made next to two commercial tools. Note that the tool on the left (the most common tool sold by nearly all the pen kit suppliers) is long and has a shallow taper. It is not a very good choice since it limits you to small brass tubes. On a larger tube, the point will eject the Play-Doh plug!

Tip: *Post-it pads make excellent epoxy mixing pads. After you use the mixed amount, tear off the top sheet and throw it out, and you have another fresh mixing surface!*

Spread some glue all over the brass tube then insert it slowly while rotating it back and forth. The objective is to try to get the gap filled with glue. Insert the tube until it is completely inside the blank. Set aside for 20 minutes to let the glue dry.

Another popular glue for gluing the brass tube is Cyanoacrylate (CA) glue, sold in many hobby and hardware stores. CA glue comes in different viscosities, and the thicker varieties are able to fill gaps better, so thick CA is the right stuff here. CA reacts with some woods and it can happen that it sets before you have the brass tube fully inserted in the wood, one of the reasons I prefer epoxy.

Polyurethane glue is also a good glue to use here. Polyurethane takes several hours to set, and it's best to let it set overnight. It expands as it dries which helps to fill the gap, but it can also set unevenly and push the brass tube out of the blank. You can prevent that by keeping an eye on it for the first half hour or so, or by using rubber bands to prevent movement. I find polyurethane very expensive to use because I invariably forget to cap the bottle and in my humid summer climate, it does not take very long for the glue to harden in the bottle.

After the glue is dry we need to square the ends of the blank to the brass tube. Most people use a pen mill for that, but you can also use a jig on a belt or disk sander. I prefer the latter method, but when I make a single pen I often use the pen mill and avoid the noise of a power tool. I can't stress enough the importance of having the ends of the blank square to the brass tube, it is an important element in making a high-quality pen. If you end up with non-square faces you run the danger of turning out-of-round (or rather non-concentric) pen barrels, and you can end up with visible gaps where it meets the hardware.

The shaft of the barrel trimmer fits a 7 mm brass tube, but our tube is bigger, so we need a shim barrel. You can purchase a shim barrel (see Tools & Materials), but it is also easy to make your own.

Check the pen barrel for any glue that snuck inside the tube despite your precautions. Use a small pocket knife to scrape out any glue you see.

The pen mill has two functions. It removes excess material right to the end of the brass tube, and it assures that the end faces are square. I like to use it just for squaring, and make sure I don't have a lot of material to trim by keeping the blank length close to the brass tube as mentioned above, so a hand operation is fine. If there's more material to remove, a power-tool like a portable electric drill is a better idea. Hold the pen blank in a vise, slide the shim tube on the pen mill shaft, and carefully cut the end faces until you *just* see the end of the brass tube pop out as a shiny ring. This is a critical step for many pens, including the Gatsby. If you trim too far, the refill may not retract completely.

Pen mills eventually get dull, especially when used in a power tool. They can be sharpened by a professional service. You can also hone them yourself. I prefer to leave the back of the cutting edges (red in the image below) alone, and just hone the large front flats (blue in the image below) using a stone or diamond file.If you have a disk or belt sander, you

8. Squaring the end faces is a critical step, you should just see the brass tube appear when you are square.

Making a Shim Barrel

When I make a shim barrel, I like to use Corian because of its stability. However, some scrap wood also works. Drill a 1¾" piece of Corian using a ⁹⁄₃₂" drill bit and glue in a 7 mm brass tube (7 mm brass tubes are available as spares from all pen kit suppliers). The brass tube helps assure a consistent diameter. Sand any protruding brass tube flush with the ends. Mount the barrel on the lathe, with another piece of 7 mm brass tube and a bushing to take up the slack, and snug up the mandrel nut. Slide the tube you want to fit right over the 7 mm tube. Turn to a consistent diameter such that the tube just slides onto the shim barrel. Having the tube right on the mandrel makes it easy and avoids having to remove the nut multiple times. File a flat on the barrel and label the shim.

A setup to make a shim barrel for larger blanks.

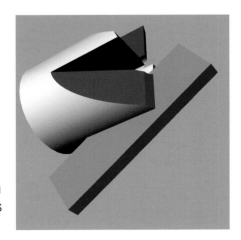

When sharpening a pen mill, only dress the large faces.

Making an Accurate Squaring Jig for your Belt or Disk Sander

An accurate squaring jig is easily made from scrap wood and an old mandrel (or an inexpensive replacement mandrel). Start with a block of wood about 1.5 x 1.5 x 2.5" (kiln-dried construction lumber is fine) and drill a ¼" hole down the middle. Try to drill as accurately as possible, parallel to the base. Insert the mandrel, exposing about 3 to 3½" at the front. The more protrusion, the longer a barrel you can square on this jig, but also the more flex it will have. If the mandrel is loose, add a drop of glue. Use a small square to make sure that the mandrel is square to the sander. If necessary, sand the bottom surface on the same sander until the protruding shaft is "dead nuts" square. Make a base plate out of ¾" plywood, about 3" x 5". To let the jig slide easily I faced mine with some scrap laminate. Now make a runner that fits into the table slot accurately. Use some suitable material, hardwood, aluminum, or a 3"–4" piece of your miter gauge bar. I used some scrap phenolic I had lying around. It can be thicker than the miter slot is deep since we will partially recess it into the jig anyway. Set the baseplate on the

sander table, and the block on it such that there is a ¼" gap between the rod and the sanding belt. Mark the location of the miter slot, and of the block.

My friend Jay Pickens came up with the following technique to square the jig horizontally. Cut a shallow dado into the baseplate, where you marked it, roughly ⅛" wider than the runner. Glue or screw the block with the mandrel to the base where you marked it. Attach the runner with a single screw in the slot, with an even gap on both sides, the screw being snug but not really tight. Set the entire assembly in the miter slot and check for easy left-right movement. Use a small square to check if the rod is square to the sanding plane horizontally—it will most likely not be. Pivot the baseplate on the screw until the mandrel is square. (This adjustment is the reason why the screw was snug but not ultra tight.) Now carefully lift out the assembly without disturbing the runner, and fill the gap around the runner with epoxy. Scrape off excess epoxy once it is dry. You can add a second screw now if you want. This jig will stay square for years!

The rod must be perfectly square to the belt sander.
Check before attaching the block to the base.

Before the runner is fixed in place carefully square
the rod horizontally.

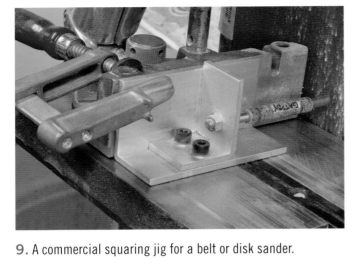

9. A commercial squaring jig for a belt or disk sander.

cannot simply put the blank on the table and square it to the belt, because you are squaring to the outer surfaces, which in the real world are *not* parallel to the brass tube, even if the drilling jig was carefully squared.

A commercial jig is available from PSI.

It clamps to a miter gauge and works well enough, if you can keep it attached securely. You have to be careful with it as it flexes easily. You can make a much better one yourself! The most important thing for this jig is that the axis be square to the belt.

Turning the blank

Now we are ready to turn! Put a light coat of wax on the mandrel and onto the bushings, to prevent accidentally gluing things together. Mount the blank on the mandrel using the bushings. Take up slack

10. Turning the barrel to the diameter of the bushings.

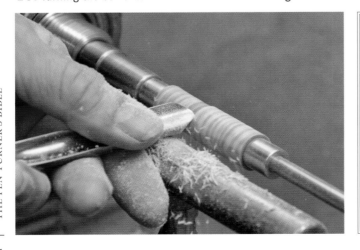

with some spare bushings, or shorten your adjustable mandrel. Tighten the mandrel nut. Bring up the tailstock, which has the 60° live center mounted in it to support the end of the mandrel. The tailstock ram should be advanced just enough so that the center turns with the mandrel. Do not overtighten the mandrel nut, or the tailstock! Adjust your tool rest close to the blank and lock it in place, maybe ⅜" below the lathe (mandrel) axis. Check that the blank clears the tool rest by spinning it by hand.

There are many good instructional books and videos on turning techniques available. A novice turner might also find some instruction at a local club or store. However, the cuts for making a pen are really easy so I'll give you the basic cut. Once you start your mounted square blank spinning it no longer looks square, but rather like a cylinder. Lay the ½" spindle gouge on the tool rest and bring the bevel (the area below the cutting edge) in contact with that virtual cylinder. This is what everyone refers to as 'rubbing the bevel' and it is an essential part of making a clean cut. Pull the tool back towards you slowly, maintaining the contact with both the tool rest and the spinning blank. At some point you will start to see small chips coming off. Now rotate the tool a little to the right and you will get more chips. Advance the tool in that position to the right till it comes off the blank. Repeat to the left. Always find that bevel first, pull back and rotate in the cutting direction. That's all there is to it! Proceed to turn the blank down until you get to the height of the bushings.

Tip: After the flat sides have been turned off and the blank is completely round, stop the lathe, unscrew the mandrel nut which may have self-tightened during the rough turning. Also back off the tailstock. Retighten both lightly. Then continue to turn to the bushings. This is an important step for many pens; omitting it may result in out-of-round barrels.

Sanding, polishing and finishing

The next step is sanding until you remove all tool marks. Your ability to turn a smooth barrel determines your starting sandpaper grit. I don't think I ever used coarser that 220 grit on pens. If you use a very coarse sand paper, it leaves very deep scratches, and all scratches need to be removed in subsequent steps. I buy rolls of cloth-backed sandpaper 1.5" wide and tear off a 6" strip. Do not wrap the sandpaper around the pen, you just trap dust and generate heat. Keep it vertical behind the pen so that sanding dust can fall off. When I started, I thought it would be a good idea to put a piece of wood behind the sandpaper because it would help make a better cylinder. It does not. Your fingers are a very sensitive gauge for temperature and roughness and provide excellent feedback. Try to avoid sanding into the bushings as much as possible, since you'll be pulling metal particles from the bushings onto the pen barrel and especially with light woods this becomes very visible. Slow the lathe down for sanding to avoid excessive heat. 800 or 1000 RPM on a VS lathe lets you sand very nicely. After all tool marks are sanded off, stop the lathe and apply some lengthwise strokes before you progress to the next grit. Step through 320, 400 and 600 grits the same way. This is the starting place for almost all finishing techniques.

When it comes to polishing and finishing, there are as many techniques out there as there are pen makers! I will show you several methods that work for me. Here we have a stabilized wood blank. You can actually put a very good polish onto one of these, but when you start using the pen the shiny surface quickly dulls. A big step beyond that is a friction polish. I like a product called Shellawax. Shellawax is a shellac-based polish that can produce a good finish with ease, and because of its simplicity we'll use that here. In later projects I will discuss other,

11. Hold the sand paper behind the blank to let the dust fall away.

12. The sanded barrel, ready for finish.

more elaborate finishing techniques that produce a harder, more durable finish.

The first step is to polish the surface to a much better finish than 600 grit. I use a product called EEE Ultrashine. It is compatible with Shellawax, and applied with a soft cotton cloth. Use a small piece of cloth to avoid getting it caught on the spinning lathe. The Ultrashine is a polish, not a finish. After a few seconds of Ultrashine wipe the surface clean. Put the lathe on its highest speed, the key is to generate high heat by friction to evaporate the solvents. Put two drops of Shellawax on a small cotton patch and apply it to the spinning lathe, moving laterally across the whole barrel. You can feel it getting hot through the

> *Tip:* Shotgun patches available in sporting goods stores are precut at 2.75" x 2.75". They are made from lint-free cotton patches and are excellent for applying finish.

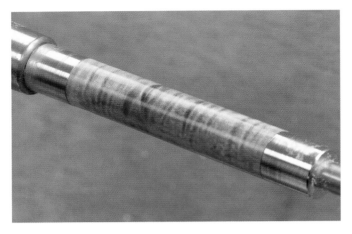

13. A little polishing with EEE Ultrashine brings out the grain and further smooths the surface.

14. After applying Shellawax as a final finish, the blank should be allowed to cool on the lathe.

application patch. Do not stop moving or you'll see rings. Part of the heat you feel is the vapor escaping through the patch. As you ease off and remove the patch you'll find the finish has dried. Add two more drops to the same application pad and repeat. Avoid over-application. I found if I went with more than two coats I risked losing it all and just creating a mess, forcing me to start over. Give the pen barrel a few minutes to cool off—do not handle while it is still warm! After that you can remove it from the lathe, still handling it gently. It's best to set the barrel aside for a few hours before assembly to allow the finish to cure.

Assembly

Pen assembly typically consists of pressing metal fittings into the turned barrels. There are many ways to accomplish that, including clamps and bench vises. The most important thing is to keep the parts' axes aligned. I have used many methods, and there are a few inexpensive methods that work better than others. A quick-grip clamp will do in a pinch, but it is hard to keep parts aligned and prevent cracking. Craft Supplies offers a jig that allows you to use your lathe and its ram. I have tried that and it works well. If you have a drill press, you can use it as an assembly press also. Just turn an anvil out of some hard material (hardwood, Corian, aluminum, etc.) and insert it in the chuck. Most pen kit suppliers offer the same lever operated pen assembly press, and it certainly works. I tried an early version that felt a little flimsy, but mostly I don't like the fact that it is horizontal. I think it is easier to keep parts aligned with gravity assist, i.e. with the parts vertical. My

Tip: *A small pocket knife makes an excellent tool to remove glue from the inside of a pen barrel. You can also use gun barrel cleaning brushes, but typically you will need many sizes since they have to be a good fit. An 8" round file is another excellent universal tool. A machinist's deburring tool like the ones shown here creates a small bevel that helps keep the parts in line during assembly.*

15. A little anvil turned from a cutoff converts the drill press into an assembly press.

16. A small arbor press makes a great assembly tool.

preferred method is a small arbor press. A 1T (one ton) arbor press has sufficient capacity to do most pens. It can be obtained inexpensively from tool suppliers like Enco or Grizzly. A protector glued to the piston avoids damaging parts. You can apply pressure in a very controlled way. Before you press in parts, make doubly sure that there is no glue left inside the tube.

Assemble according to the kit manufacturer's instructions. Look at the grain and decide which end should be forward. Press the front fitting into

the lower end of the barrel. Look at the grain again to decide where you want the clip to be. You don't want the clip to intrude on or obscure the nicest grain. On the other hand, the clip can be used to hide a tiny defect in the finish. Press the upper fitting into the other end. Screw the tip on. Insert the refill and spring, and screw the transmission into the upper fitting. Apply some torque screwing it in so it remains seated when you operate the pen. Press on the upper finial, and you are done! Sit back and admire your creation!

Section II:
Easy Projects

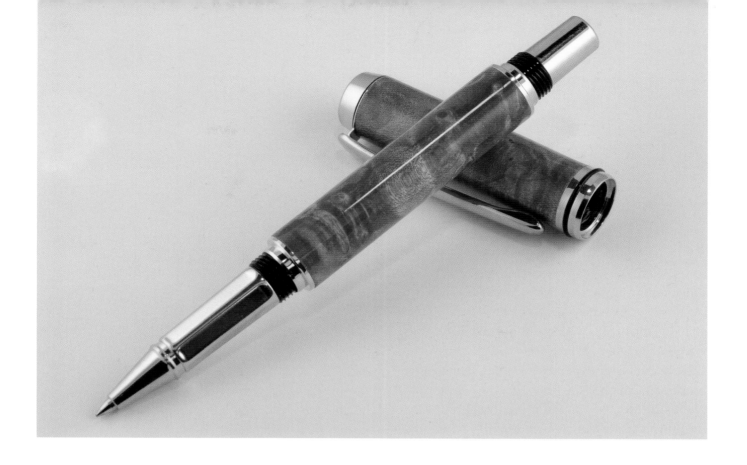

5. A Medium-Size Rollerball Pen

The Baron pen is a medium-size rollerball or fountain pen, available in several variations that are similar but not all are 100% compatible. Different suppliers offer the kit in various plating. The Baron version from arizonasilhouette.com and the Navigator from Woodcraft have the advantage of having no taper in the barrel, which reduces the chance for assembly errors. Some of the other versions have slight tapers and somewhat better lines. Craft Supplies USA sells a version that looks the same but has larger diameter barrels overall.

Burl wood adds some drama to pens. For this pen I have selected a maple burl. In burl, the grain runs wild and changes direction, so your tools will encounter face grain as well as end grain. Sharp tools and light cuts are in order when turning burl!

Start by laying out all the components and familiarizing yourself with the kit. Use the brass tubes to lay out the pen on the blank, leaving about ¼" waste on each half. If you want to keep the grain aligned, mark the center of the blank across the cut line. Grain alignment is not terribly important with screw cap pens, and certainly not with burl but it is not a bad habit to get into. Cut the blanks, and drill each without exiting the wood to avoid a blowout. This is very important with burl! Now use the band saw to cut off the waste to the length of the tubes plus a smidgen.

Tools & Materials

- Lathe and standard tooling
- Baron rollerball pen kit (arizonasilhouette.com)
- Bushings for Baron pen
- Pen mill and shim barrels (make your own)
- Burl pen blank
- $\frac{25}{64}$" drill bit
- $\frac{15}{32}$" drill bit
- Thin and medium CA glue and accelerator
- Micro-mesh kit 1,500–12,000 mesh

1. Use the brass tubes to mark cutting lines on the blank. Mark the center cut.

Roughen the brass tubes with a bit of sandpaper, plug the end with Play-Doh, or dental base plate wax, and glue the tubes. With burls, polyurethane glue is a good glue to use since you want good coverage. Polyurethane glue expands as it dries. During that process, it can push the brass tubes out of the blank. Photo 2 shows two ways to prevent such shifts. Let the polyurethane glue dry overnight.

Remove all traces of glue from inside of the brass barrels. Square the ends until you *just* see the brass tube, using a pen mill or squaring jig for your sander with appropriately sized homemade shim barrels. You can also buy ready made sleeves from arizonasilhouette.com. Coat the bushings with paste wax since we will use a CA finish, this discourages glue from sticking to the bushings. Because I have it on my bench, I use Renaissance wax, but household paste wax works just fine.

Mount the blanks on the lathe and turn to the bushings. Do not overtighten the mandrel nut or the tailstock. The tailstock should just support the end of the mandrel and not exert axial pressure. The ½" spindle-gouge is all you need. Make sure it is sharp and take light cuts, especially near the ends and as you get close to the bushings. Always find the bevel first; if you don't and use a scraping cut you run the danger of ripping out a piece of the burl. Once the barrel is round, loosen the mandrel nut and the tailstock and retighten gently. While the blank is non-round, the interrupted cut has a tendency to tighten the mandrel nut. This is an important step since too much end pressure can put a bend into the mandrel and make your turning come out eccentric, often

2. With polyurethane glue you need to keep the brass tubes from moving as the glue cures. A rubber band or some pins do the job.

3. Two barrels mounted on the mandrel using the bushings.

(incorrectly) referred to as out-of-round. For the final cuts I use the side of the fingernail grind. This uses a part of the tool not dulled yet. The edge, where it contacts the wood, runs at approximately a 45° angle to the axis. With the bevel rubbing, this cut is about the same as using a skew and you can make a very fine surface that does not need a lot of sanding. You can even lay the bevel on the bushing and come off the bushing into the wood.

Sand to 400 or 600 grit to remove all of the tool marks. Avoid sanding the bushings and carrying metal dust into the light wood. Sanding is best done around 1000 RPM or slower. Use calipers to measure the diameter of the barrel close to the bushings. The Baron fittings are 0.482" and 0.535". The wood should be that, or just below, to allow the slight buildup of the finish.

We will use CA glue as finish. It is a tough finish that can be polished to a high gloss. There are many ways to use CA to finish wood. I will show you one method I use. Not all CA's are equally suited to finishing. I have tried several brands, and found what works for me. I like the Stickfast brand Klingspor distributes, along with the aerosol accelerator. Slow a variable speed (VS) lathe down all the way and add a few drops of thin CA to the sanding dust trapped by the sandpaper. Rub this slurry into the surface, it will fill any small cracks in the burl. Now sand back to bare wood with 400-grit paper. You don't want the dried slurry to hide the grain! Using a discarded poly bag from the pen kit to protect your finger, spread some medium CA over the barrel while the lathe is turning slowly. Smear it out evenly. A few seconds will allow the CA to flow a little and even out, then squirt some accelerator on it. Apply a second coat of CA in the same fashion. Trial and error will tell you if you need a 3rd or even 4th coat. Once the CA is dry, use a skew, laid flat, to scrape the high spots off the CA. You should get very fine white shavings. The objective is to get about 50–70% of the surface dull. Low spots will show up shiny. The skew, laid flat, allows excellent control and minute removal. If you went straight to sandpaper, your soft, unsupported fingers would tend to follow the surface, hitting high as well as low spots. The scraping skew just touches high spots.

Now switch to 400 grit paper and sand till all shiny spots are gone. Should you break through to wood, apply another CA layer. Stop the lathe and sand the surfaces with lengthwise strokes while turning the spindle by hand.

4. Cutting with the side of the fingernail-ground spindle gouge lets you achieve a fine finish that requires little sanding.

5. Use calipers to check the turned diameter rather than relying on the bushings which will wear over time.

6. Use a poly bag to evenly spread medium CA.

7. Scrape the cured CA with a skew laid flat on the tool rest.

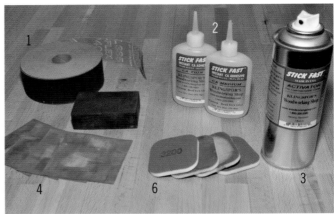

8. Supply for a CA finish: (1) sand paper, (2) CA thin and medium, (3) accelerator, (4) micro-mesh sheets with (5) rubber backing block or (6) micro-mesh pads.

9. After taking the barrels off the lathe there is often some glue burr that must be removed.

10. Removing glue burr.

Micro-mesh polishing pads are available in thin sheets to be used with a rubber backing block, and in double sided pads on a foam carrier. I have better luck with the pads. Starting with 1500 mesh, polish the barrels until there are no marks from the previous grade visible. Use a 1000 RPM lathe speed. Slap the pads against your other hand to knock out dust as it fills the pad. Finish with longitudinal strokes again, while the lathe is stopped. Repeat this using the finer meshes all the way up to 12,000. Again, if dull spots start appearing as you go through this, you have probably broken though the CA and need to go back and apply another layer.

Take the barrels off the mandrel. You'll probably find that there is some glue burr sticking out at the end of the barrel. I use one of the medium micro-mesh pads (like 3200) to polish the end of the barrel until it is gone. Assemble the pen according to the instructions. What a beauty!

6. A Large Fountain Pen

The Statesman pen is a very large and hefty pen. It's also available in a somewhat less ornate version as the Gentleman's pen. The construction is identical, so the same turned barrels can be assembled not only into a fountain or rollerball pen, but also in two decoration levels. For this pen we'll use a manmade stone sold under various names like Tru-stone or Gemstone. I will use the Gemstone name here. The pen blanks are available in various sizes, from $^{11}/_{16}$" to $^{7}/_{8}$". The final turned diameter of the cap is .650". $^{11}/_{16}$" = .688", so there is only .038" room for drilling error. You're well advised to use a blank of at least $^{3}/_{4}$". A supersized $^{7}/_{8}$" blank is a good idea for this pen unless you are able to drill with very high precision.

Gemstone pen blanks vary in hardness. Malachite is one of the softer ones. Chilean lapis is one of the hardest blanks I have encountered. With any of these, expect to sharpen your turning tools several times within one pen. But the material *can* be worked with regular HSS tools, it just takes patience. The results are worth it.

After familiarizing yourself with the instructions and identifying the parts, lay out the barrels on the blank, adding about $^{3}/_{8}$" at the ends. Gemstone does break out if you drill through! Because of the larger point on the huge $^{37}/_{64}$" bit I add more than the $^{1}/_{4}$" I use on smaller pens.

Tools & Materials

- Lathe and standard tooling
- Statesman fountain pen kit from Craft Supply USA (CSU)
- Bushings for Statesman pen
- $^{3}/_{4}$" pen mill and shim barrels (make your own)
- Oversize gemstone blank (malachite)
- $^{37}/_{64}$" drill bit
- $^{15}/_{32}$" drill bit
- Micro-mesh kit 1,500–12,000 mesh

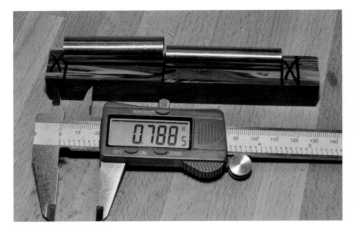

1. Lay out the cuts including some waste. Choose the larger end of the blank for the cap.

2. Squaring the blanks is even more important with large diameter pens.

Cut the blanks on the band saw. If your large drill bit is in good condition, you can drill the cap barrel with only that ³⁷⁄₆₄" bit. To be on the safe side, start with a ⅜" drill, then follow with a ½", and finally use the ³⁷⁄₆₄" without moving the table.

Cut the blanks to the length of the brass tubes plus a smidgen. Plug the end of the brass tube with Play-Doh, or dental plate wax, and glue in the tubes with epoxy. Because of the large diameter, out-of-square effects are emphasized, so pay extra attention to squaring the ends. If you use a sanding jig check it with an engineer's square, and use a barrel trimmer and the same shim tube to double check your squared blank. A single turn of the tool should make a nice circle. Photo 2 shows the squared blanks. The blank I used measured between .749" and .788", note the amount of material left, using the ¾" barrel trimmer ring as reference. Also notice that I have transferred the center marking to the inside of the brass tube which will come in handy at assembly time. This is not necessary on the main barrel since it tapered.

The Statesman's pen features a smooth transition from the main barrel to the metal end (finial). This is the most critical diameter to turn. It must be the correct diameter and concentric with the brass tube. Fingers are very sensitive and will pick up any step to the metal. Because of that make sure that the mandrel runs true. A surprisingly sensitive test is running the mandrel at medium speed and using a fingernail to feel for vibration. Pick the end of the mandrel

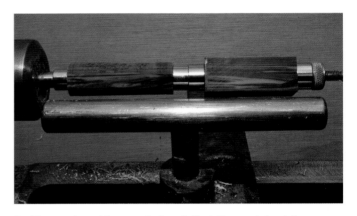

3. The cap barrel is mounted such that the mark is at the tailstock end.

that has less vibration/runout to place the smallest bushing. Note that I have also mounted the cap barrel 'backwards', so that the clip end is in the middle and the center is at the tailstock end of the mandrel. I consider the diameter next to the centerband more critical than the clip end.

Turning gemstone is no different than turning wood, other than generally slower. The ½" spindle gouge is still a good tool to use. The material comes off in long ribbons that wrap themselves around the turning. Just keep going, clearing off when you can't see what you are doing. The stone is abrasive, so dress your gouge frequently. Once the barrels are round, stop the lathe, loosen the mandrel nut and the tailstop and retighten them gently. The mandrel nut should be just tight enough so that the blank does not spin, and the tailstock just enough to support the end of the

4. The material comes off in long ribbons that you need to clear off after stopping the lathe.

5. When assembling the cap, screw the cap fitting on and look for grain alignment.

to a uniform surface. You can never remove deeper marks with finer grits, they will just become more visible later, and they will not disappear magically! Finish each grit with lengthwise strokes. After 400 grit switch to micro-mesh. Work through all the grits, again finishing each grade with lengthwise strokes, all the way up to 12,000 mesh.

Remove any burr from the brass tube edge, in particular for the cap tube. The pen kit has a Delrin sleeve that lines the tube, and if there is a burr on the tube, it will raise a shaving that can prevent the center fitting from seating properly. The machinist's deburring tool comes in very handy for that.

Assemble the pen by pressing the parts in the following sequence to achieve best grain alignment. Screw the nib into the front fitting and find the best grain or pattern. Partially insert the fitting into the main body. Carefully unscrew the nib and press the fitting in all the way. Don't forget the trim ring, large flat towards the pen body. The main body finial is a two-part piece. Do *not* separate them before assembly. Press the finial assembly in next. Then partially press the Delrin liner sleeve into the cap end marked as center. Add the center band fitting and screw it onto the pen. Rotate the cap for the best grain alignment (Photo 5) Unscrew the complete cap assembly, being careful not to rotate the center band, and press it in. Finally, add the clip and cap finial, lining the clip up with the least interesting grain, or to hide any tiny defect you might find. What a beautiful pen!

mandrel. If it is too loose the live center will not turn with the mandrel, or will make a screaming noise. Give the main barrel a pleasing shape, starting fairly straight from the larger bushing, and then gently tapering down to the smaller bushing. I like giving the cap barrel a straight shape, the pen is already heavy enough, I don't want to add more weight. Use calipers to check the very end of the pen body barrel, it should be 0.525".

On gemstone, there is no need to apply a finish! You can just polish the pen to a high gloss. Start with sandpaper, a grit that will allow you to remove all tool marks. I just do 400 grit, you may want to start at 320 or 220 grit, whatever it takes to come

7. The Fine Points

This chapter might also be called 'dealing with the real world'. In theory, our lathe mandrels run true, there is no slop when the bushings or barrels are mounted, bushings are always perfect diameter and all parts and fittings are concentric. Unfortunately, much of this is just not true in reality, and we have to find ways to deal with it. Luckily there are ways to reduce or hide imperfections due to these real-life limitations.

The trouble stems from trying to make perfect transitions from parts we turn, to manufactured fittings we buy in the kits. Some kits are harder to get perfect than others. We want to have the turned barrel transition smoothly into the fitting, without noticeable step up or down. A step up from barrel to fitting is worse, because the edges of the metal fittings typically have very sharp corners that can be felt easily. So one point to remember is if we run into equipment limitations for some reason, it's better to have the barrel oversize at the transition than undersize. If the barrel is oversize you can polish a tiny bevel at the end and it will be much less noticeable than leaving it square.

Let's look at the complete system. Start with the headstock of the lathe. There should be no marks inside the Morse-taper. If there are nicks, they should be carefully removed. A Morse-taper reamer can dress up a poor surface. Go very easy, do not do this under power, you don't want to remove a lot of material. If you use a collet chuck, like I do, to mount the mandrel, make sure the collet surfaces remain clean every time you take out the collet. To check if a mandrel runs true, a dial test indicator on a magnetic base comes in handy (Photo 2). Rotate the mandrel by hand and observe the runout, the variation during one rotation. There should be very little runout next to the headstock, barely observable on the scale. In general, runout near .003", or less, is OK. Then measure next to the tail stock. Because the mandrel is supported there, there should be minimal runout. If there is more than .003" make sure there is no dirt trapped between the live center and the mandrel, or

1. Use a Morse-taper reamer to clean up a damaged Morse-taper that has internal marks and burrs.

2. A dial indicator or a dial test indicator (shown) can be used to measure runout on a mandrel.

that the center is not worn. If neither is the case and you still get too much runout, change the mandrel.

Lastly, measure in the center of the mandrel. If there is unacceptable runout here but not at the ends the mandrel is bowed. You can often repair it by hand by pulling the high spot against the tool rest gently (Photo 3). Mark the high spot first so when you re-measure you can see if you have made an improvement or gone too far.

Next, come the bushings. Bushings are wear and tear items; you can't avoid a little sanding, or hitting occasionally with the turning tool. I think slightly

3. After finding a high spot you can pull the mandrel carefully against the tool rest to straighten it.

undersized bushings are actually not bad. Often they start out oversize from the manufacturer. Check the diameter of a new bushing and compare it to the metal fitting that will go next to it. I finish my pens with CA, and CA has a certain amount of build-up. I find it more important to measure the turned barrel and be a little under, then add CA and end up right on or even a little over. So a worn bushing is actually desirable. Once you have CA on the bushing it's actually good during sanding since you will have less chance to pull metal particles into your turning.

Tip: *You can check your mandrel even without measuring equipment. Of course you can't get quantitative information on runout, but you can tell if the center is much worse than the ends by holding a fingernail against the spinning mandrel. To mark the high spot, lay a pencil on the tool rest and gently touch it to the spinning mandrel. You will see the pencil mark extends only part way around, and the location marks the high spot. Put the high spot in the back (facing away from the tool rest) and pull the mandrel towards the tool rest as shown in Photo 3.*

Bushings and mandrels should match. Different manufacturers have different standards. A bushing from Berea will be loose on a Penn State mandrel. A Penn State bushing may not fit onto a Berea mandrel. Perhaps you can tolerate the slight slop in one case, but you would have to ream out the bushing in the other.

Sometimes the kit's brass tubes will be loose on even brand new bushings. I find that very annoying. I have observed differences of .008" between a bushing's small diameter and the brass tube it is supposed to fit. In that case, a small piece of brass shim stock can be wrapped around a bushing to improve the fit.

To keep the loaded mandrel running true, it is important that the barrel ends are squared. The pen mill usually assures that. A sanding jig needs to be checked occasionally using a pen mill. (See Photo 2 in the previous chapter) Secondly, the axial load on the mandrel should be kept low, which means the live center should be just tight enough to support the mandrel. The mandrel nut should be just tight enough to let you turn without the barrels spinning. Both of these should be reset after rough turning because rough turning can self-tighten them.

The most difficult kits to get perfect are pens that feature a smooth transition from barrel to fitting with no adjacent ornamentation. Any kind of ornamental feature, generally a decorative ring or a step in the fitting will effectively hide small inaccuracies. The Statesman (Chapter 6) pen is a perfect example. At the cap center band, there is a decorative ring. At the clip end, there is the rim of the clip and the finial has a different slope from the barrel. Together these will also hide small inaccuracies. On the main barrel, at the front end, the double step of the trim ring makes it somewhat tolerant. Here it is important to be slightly high, if anything, and break the edge by polishing a small bevel. The upper end of the main barrel is the most critical—a seamless transition from barrel to fitting. Of course it is a little difficult to measure the very edge of a sloping barrel, so be careful positioning calipers.

One way to deal with inaccuracies and tough transitions is to exaggerate. Close is bad and objectionable, but really oversize and sloping into the fitting, or rounded over, hides diameter problems. Photo 4 shows this technique employed deliberately. In the ivory pen (Chapter 10) I wanted to increase diameter by about .035". Left square, the diameter mismatch would look terrible. Rounded over it is barely noticeable. The same goes for the slope at a transition. It looks best if the slope of the barrel end is the same as the slope of the fitting. I like blending shapes smoothly. I will note these shape and slope features when we make the Perfect Fit pen in Chapter 8.

Lastly I'd like to mention grain alignment between barrels. There are some pens where this is important such as a click pen made with two barrels. Once assembled, they never change relative orientation. Twist pens are already a little less critical, most

people like to keep the grain aligned when the pen is closed. For pens where the diameter changes in the center, in many cases this is not important—but it can be, depending on the material. For example angle cut woods or dymondwood will look odd unless the grain is aligned. Pens with caps often have multi-start threads. That means, there are three or four orientations possible. I like to make sure there is at least one orientation where the grain is aligned, and I will put the cap on such that the grain matches. So for fountain pens, first I make sure the nib is aligned with the nicest grain on the barrel. Then I add the cap so that the grain matches. Lastly, and that is true for all pens, I orient the clip such that it either covers any tiny defect, or that it goes over the most uninteresting grain.

4. A barrel turned oversize and gently rounded over to the fittings is barely noticeable.

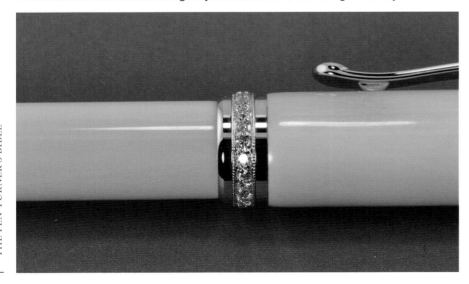

8. Perfect Fit Ballpoint Pen

The Perfect Fit pen is an interesting pen since it can be set up as a ballpoint as well as a pencil. The same conversion cartridge, with a little bit of work, can be used on other pen models that use a Parker-style refill. However, the Perfect Fit Convertible works without modification. Because it uses a different, easier-moving mechanism than most other kit pens it lends itself to a pencil better than others.

We use an acrylic acetate pen blank here. There are many plastic pen blanks available, and they have some different properties, but in principle, all can be used with the same techniques. One of the common properties is that they melt when they get too hot. How hot they can get before melting varies by material. Acrylic acetate can be taken to higher temperatures than some of the older resins you may find.

When plastics are drilled, it is best to slow the speed down to around 1000-RPM. When you start drilling at first you generate fairly rigid ribbons. As you proceed and the drill bit gets hot the ribbons become soft. It is time to stop and let the bit cool if that happens or you can create a mess that ruins the pen blank and gunks up your drill bit.

If you get a chance to hand-select acrylic blanks take advantage of that. Check blanks out for pattern on all sides. The blanks in Photo 1 are the same, but obviously the one in front will result in a more exciting pen.

Tools & Materials

- Lathe and standard tooling
- Perfect Fit Convertible pen kit from Berea
- Bushings for Convertible pen
- Pen mill and shim barrels (make your own)
- Acrylic acetate pen blank
- Acrylic crafts paint to match the blank
- 'S' drill bit
- 'P' drill bit
- B mandrel
- Micro-mesh kit 1,500–12,000 mesh
- One micron diamond paste

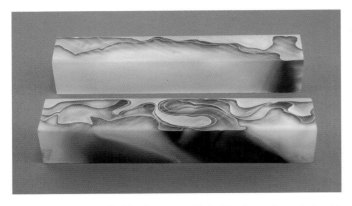

1. Like wood, acrylic blanks vary widely. The lower barrel should produce a more exciting pen.

2. Acrylic becomes transparent when it is turned thin. You can change the color significantly by painting the brass tube.

As plastics get thin, they become more translucent. You can buy some brass tubes that are bright nickel or dark plated, or painted white, or you can paint them yourself. But you can also see gaps in the glue through the plastic at times. The best way to avoid this is to paint the inside of the drilled hole with a suitable color. Your color choice can change the look of the pen. An example demonstrating the effect is shown in Photo 2. The brass tube was striped red and white and pushes the orange acrylic from nearly yellow to deep red. I use acrylic craft paint available from hobby stores. It comes in many colors and is very inexpensive. Most craft stores sell these paints in a separate aisle, not near the artists' paints. I have used the cheapest and the most expensive, which is still only roughly $2, and only buy the premium paints now since I usually get good coverage with a single coat.

Lay out the barrels on the blank, making use of the best pattern. Leave ⅜" extra at the end to avoid having the drill bit exit. Cut on the band saw and drill at 1000 RPM. The choice of drill bit type is not too

critical for plastics but it should be sharp to reduce heating. The recommended drill bits for this pen are ¹¹⁄₃₂" and "O", but because of the thickness of the paint, I am using slightly larger sizes "S" and "P". Cut to length as usual. The front barrel length is critical. If it is too short, the refill will not retract completely.

Berea has two methods in their instructions for making the upper barrel. One method is to start with a full-length cap barrel and then cut a tenon down to the brass tube. The other starts with a shortened barrel that leaves a piece of brass tube protruding. I always start with a full-length blank. Blow out dust from the inside of the blanks and paint the inside. A Q-tip makes a good applicator (Photo 3). Let it dry overnight or use a hair dryer to accelerate drying. Glue in the brass tube with epoxy.

Mount it on the lathe using the bushings. Here the smaller (front) tube will fit directly onto the mandrel, the bushings have no step. I mount the upper barrel in reverse because I want the critical diameter near the headstock. Turning acrylic is a little different from turning wood, but our standard ½" spindle gouge works quite well.

The pen shape is to some degree dictated by the kit. Let me preface this by saying there is no absolute right or wrong way; 'right' is very subjective. You can turn wild shapes and if they please you, great! To me it looks good if the fittings match the barrels in diameter and slope at the junctions. This means that for the upper barrel, the shape should be a straight barrel of the diameter of the bushing, or rather the center band (A in Photo 4). This is actually a necessity because we will cut a tenon later, and if you did not keep a constant diameter you would not be able to match the center band. In the upper half, as you

3. Painting the inside of the barrel prevents the brass tube and the glue from showing through.

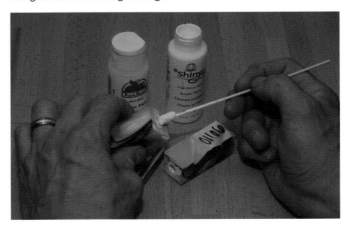

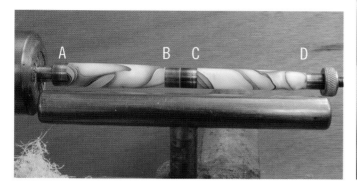

4. A flowing shape makes an elegant pen.

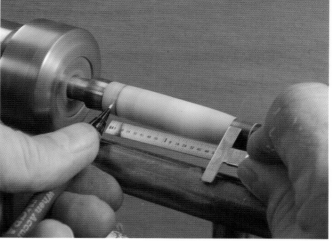

5. Mark the shoulder for the tenon.

approach the finial (B in Photo 4) turn a gentle slope towards the bushing. Note that the finial itself does not have straight sides but is sloped. You will find the barrel will flow into this slope smoothly. For the lower barrel, near the center (C) I like keeping a constant diameter, but the pen can have a little barrel shape also, if you prefer, and still meet the criteria I laid out. In the last ¾" or so (D) turn a gentle slope towards the bushing and you'll find that the slightly tapered ends up about right to smoothly flow into the tip.

Acrylics do not need any finish; you can just polish to a high gloss. Again, all tool marks need to be removed by sanding, at or up to 400 or 600 grit. Follow by lengthwise strokes. At this point, or after the first grades of micro-mesh, we need to cut a tenon for the center band. The tenon is best cut after the 1500, 1800, or 2400 micro-mesh polish. If we cut it before sanding there is a tendency to roll over the sharp corner of the tenon. If we cut the tenon at the very end, often it leaves an unsightly burr, which we then have to back off through a few grades of polish. And yes, that happens; I've been known to forget and polish all the way through. Carefully mark the length from the finial end. The length of the remaining acrylic is critical for the pen to work properly. It needs to be between 1¾" and 1⅞". The length of the tenon itself is not critical, so you can make up for any prior inaccuracy in length. Use a parting tool to cut all the way down to the brass tube.

You can follow the polishing sequence from the previous chapter using micro-mesh. I will use micro-mesh wet here. It took me a long time to try wet polishing since I am not thrilled with water around the lathe. If you have easy access to water in your shop, this works well for acrylics as well as CA. Put a rag across your lathe bed to catch drips. Dip the 1500 micro-mesh in water and polish. It will quickly build up white slurry; avoid letting it dry. A single wetting will generally do. Stop the lathe and do lengthwise

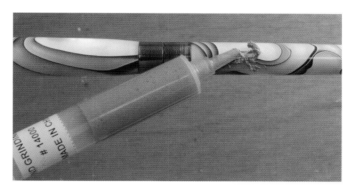

6. Diamond paste adds an extra luster.

strokes, use the rag to dry the blank and remove any remaining slurry. Work up through the grades to 12,000 and you should get a fantastic gloss.

I don't follow this with any of the plastic polishes. But I have found a product that seems to add yet a little more gloss: diamond polishing paste. It is available from lapidary suppliers or on eBay. See Resources on page 141. Squeeze about a ½" length onto the barrel, and rub it on with lengthwise strokes using a soft cloth or gun barrel patch while rotating the spindle by hand. Then polish it off using a clean area of the cloth. Finer diamond polishes are available though for me it's hard to discern further improvement.

Press all the parts in according to the instructions. If the center band is loose, use a tiny bit of epoxy. I never use CA glue on a finished pen. With epoxy, if you get any squeeze-out, you can simply wipe it off without leaving any residue. You can't do that with CA. Also, CA in enclosed spaces takes a long time to cure, on the order of days! During that time it releases a vapor that leaves a white film on plated parts in enclosed spaces.

To set the pen up as a pencil simply remove the refill and drop in a conversion cartridge available from Berea Hardwoods or their distributors.

Three examples of antler pens.

9. Antler Cigar Pen

Antler makes beautiful pens and is relatively simple to work. Unlike horns, antlers are shed annually, so no animal has to die. Although hunting friends may supply you with material in exchange for a pen, it is often challenging to find a section suitable for pens in such material. There are many species of deer, and their antlers vary in terms of suitability for pens. Photo 1 shows a number of different antler sections obtained from a variety of sources. Most antlers have a porous center section, and a hard outer surface we'll call enamel. Note that the ratio of porous center to enamel varies. White Tail deer, common in the North East where I live, is usually challenging since it has little enamel. Sambar and axis deer antler work very well for pens. They work very well for pens, because they have straight sections, and a thick enamel layer. Many pen kit suppliers have antler available that works well for pens. Depending on the section you choose you can make different looking pens. Let's start with an easy one. I will choose two pieces of antler that are straight and are not too porous at the center.

Antler has a smell that takes some getting used to. It's an organic material, and if you are sensitive to smells wear an appropriate breathing mask. I am not aware of health issues related to antler dust, but at least a dust mask is advisable. Choose sections by holding the pen tubes next to the antler, mark cut locations, and cut on the band saw, ⅜" longer than

THE PEN TURNER'S BIBLE

Tools & Materials

- Lathe and standard tooling
- Cigar pen kit
- Mandrel, bushings for cigar pen
- Pen mill and shim barrels (make your own)
- Antler
- ²⁵⁄₆₄" drill bit
- Abralon pads, 500–4000 mesh
- Cotton polishing wheel and white diamond compound
- Hydrogen peroxide
- Potassium permanganate

1. Antler has many different shapes, textures and cross-sections affecting suitability for pens.

2. Using an electric drill with a pen mill to square up a pen barrel.

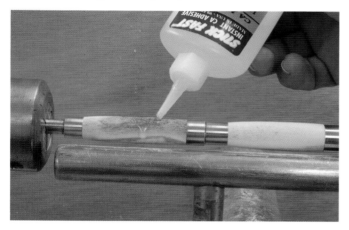

3. Fill porous sections of the antler with thin, followed by medium CA.

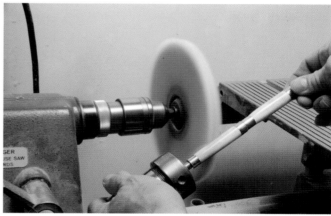

4. A polishing wheel lets you achieve a great sheen directly without the need for a finish.

the tubes. Drill using the ²⁵⁄₆₄" drill bit without exiting. Then cut the closed end. Because the end surfaces on an irregular blank are usually off square, cut a little longer than you would cut a regular wood blank, so you have enough material to square the ends. Trim on the belt sander using a squaring jig, or use a barrel trimmer in an electric drill. Both barrels are length-sensitive, do not shorten the brass tubes, trim until you *just* touch the end of the brass tube.

There are many ways to mix up blanks and bushings on a cigar pen because both tubes are the same diameter but different lengths, and the bushings have four diameters. The simple way is to line up the bushings by size. One is the smallest, four the largest. Mount on the mandrel in the following order: Bushing one, long blank, bushing three, bushing two, short blank, bushing four. This orients the tip at the headstock, and the center band at the tailstock.

The ½" spindle gouge again works well. Turn to the bushings, giving the pen the shape you like. Here I make a fairly slim pen to my liking. Carefully look at the surface and see if any porous center has become exposed. If so, dribble some thin followed by medium CA on that area. The thin CA penetrates easier, and it seems to help the medium CA fill the gaps better. Sand up to 400 or 600 grit to get rid of all tool marks. Again, inspect for areas that need filling and repeat the procedure until you have a solid surface. I generally do not add a finish to antler, I just polish it. However, you may decide to use a CA finish as described in Chapter 5. My preferred polishing pads for antler are Abralon, an open-cell polishing pad. Use them at 1000 RPM and avoid getting them hot. Run through the grades, finishing each grade with lengthwise strokes. I then take the barrels to a cotton polishing wheel and polish with white diamond compound to give them that extra shine. I leave the blanks on the mandrel, which is still in my Beall

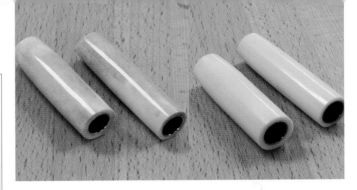

5. On the left, the barrels as turned. On the right, the barrels have turned white after a soaking in hydrogen peroxide for two days.

6. Correct alignment of your drill lets you preserve some bark on the pen which adds a lot of character.

7. Potassium Permanganate can restore faded bark to a dark brown.

Tip: Gray or splotchy antler can be returned to white. The discoloration is a sign of the antler being a little old, probably having been left outside for a while after it was shed. You can often restore it to white by soaking the finished barrel in hydrogen peroxide. The pharmacy variety is quite weak, and it turns into water over time, so use a fresh bottle, and soak for a couple of days until it becomes white. Note that antler will swell up some with the soaking— allow some days to dry out and come back to the turned dimensions after you soak.

collet chuck. This gives me something to hold while polishing. Instead of Abralon you can also use micromesh up to 12,000 mesh.

Assemble by following the kit instructions.

I like leaving some of the outer surface of the antler (we'll call it bark) showing on the pen. For that, we need to drill very close to the surface, and it helps if we also make the pen a little fat. I chose a piece of antler that had a little curvature, call it a banana shape, and a somewhat gnarly bark surface. Cut and mount in a drill vise, clamping the two ends and middle in the vise. When you look from the open end of the vise you see the side of the banana. Now comes the tricky part: The drill bit needs to enter the flat part on top with some space around it for the bushing, and you need to avoid breaking through on the inner curved part of the banana. I do this by lowering the drill bit and moving the drill vise back, sighting whether I can make the hole.

It is not always possible. Sometimes a little shimming can help. It is tricky if the banana is very bent! It may be helpful to mark where you want the drill bit to enter. Or, if you have an x-y vise like me, just move the vise back till the drill bit lines up with the blank.

After that, everything is the same as before. You do not have the option of doing a CA finish because it is hard to keep the CA out of the bark area. If you have some filling to do, have a paper towel ready for a quick wipe if some CA runs into the bark. Start with a fat shape and judge what shape you can get away with while preserving the bark. The photo on page 42 shows three antler pens with very different looks.

Tip: If the bark color has faded, it can be restored by soaking the blank in potassium permanganate solution. Potassium permanganate is a purple salt used as an iron remover in water treatment systems. You can find it on eBay. A few ounces will last you forever. Strong suggestion; wear gloves when using it! Potassium permanganate will stain your skin brown and it will not wash off.

10. Ivory Pen

Working with ivory presents some special challenges. The material itself is not really any harder to work than antler. The main distinction is cost. Ivory for a pen can cost more than $100! So lots of extra care is necessary to avoid damage during construction that can lead to cracking later. Trade in elephant ivory has been illegal for years, but documented pre-ban elephant ivory can be obtained legally. Other non-restricted sources of ivory are mammoth ivory, or ivory from teeth like hippo or warthog. None of it is inexpensive! I will use mammoth ivory for this pen. Mammoth ivory is over 10,000 years old and is found in the Siberian tundra.

The key for working ivory is to avoid stress, mechanical as well as thermal. An ivory pen is not a knock-around pen, it should be kept in a reasonably stable environment in terms of heat and humidity because ivory can shrink and expand which can lead to cracking. Cracks usually start at the ends or at tiny internal fractures. Knowing this, we can take some extra care to avoid problems. First I will choose a pen with a thick wall, even turn the barrel larger than the bushings and round over the ends. Secondly, we will use flexible glue and try to not have full glue coverage. The gap should aid in allowing some movement. Third, fittings are not pressed in, but rather the tubes are enlarged and fittings are glued.

The kit I chose is the Venus kit. When made to the bushing dimensions, the wall thickness in the cap is about .040". We will increase the wall thickness by about .015". The main body has a taper to it and the wall thickness changes from about .055" at the lower end to a little under .040" at the upper end. By using two large trim rings instead of the two

Tools & Materials

- Lathe and standard tooling
- Venus pen kit from Craft Supply USA
- Spare, large, main-body trim ring
- Mandrel and bushings for Venus pen
- Pen mill and shim barrels (make your own)
- Ivory: at least ⅝" square by 2" and ⅝" square by 2¼"
- 12.5 mm and 10.5 mm drill bits
- Micro-Mesh

1. Glue a wasteblock to the ivory to increase the safety margin when drilling.

2. Knock the corners off on the belt sander to avoid stress to the barrels during roughing cuts.

sizes that come with the kit, we'll eliminate the taper and keep a constant thicker wall of .057". The second large trim ring can come from another kit, and can usually be obtained as a spare from the store.

To keep ivory cool make sure you use very sharp tools. From saw, to drill bit, to your lathe tools, and don't rush. Because ivory is expensive try to buy exactly the length you need. If this means you end up with a piece that does not have the extra ⅜" we usually add to avoid the drill bit exiting the blank, glue on a waste piece to drill into (Photo 1).

Drill a little at a time and allow the drill bit and blank to cool off. Cut the waste block off on the band saw. Make sure the brass tubes slide in smoothly and don't bind! The adhesive I use is E6000 which is flexible. Roughen the brass tube a little with sandpaper and apply two strips of adhesive to the brass tube and to the inside of the blank using a wood stick. Line up the adhesive strips and push the brass tubes in straight without the usual twisting motion. The idea is to provide a bond but still allow for some movement. Allow to dry overnight so that the glue deep inside the tube has time to cure. At the ends, the glue dries much faster, but I know from experience that it is

3. Flood the barrel ends with CA before turning.

easy to push the tube out accidentally if you don't allow sufficient curing time. Square the ends. To reduce the possibility of the shock of roughing cuts creating micro-cracks, knock the corners off the blanks on the belt sander (Photo 2) Carefully flood the end surfaces with thin CA (Photo 3). Micro-tips (very thin-nozzle accessories sold for CA bottle tips) work very well for this. The idea is to let CA wick into any micro-cracks we may not see at the ends. Re-square the blanks, removing most of the CA that dried on the surface. The shop made tool on page 54 works very well for this.

Do not turn to the bushings, but use calipers to turn the cap barrel to .600" diameter. Round over the ends to the bushings. The standard main body bushings are .480" and .512". We want to avoid the taper, so either use a second .512" bushing if you have a second set, or again use calipers to turn to .512". Avoid rounding over the end in the latter case when polishing. Sand and polish using micro-mesh, making sure the blanks do not get hot. I use dry micro-mesh on ivory. I don't want to take any chances with a liquid that may stain the expensive ivory!

When assembling the pen we again want to avoid stress. Usually the fittings are pressed into the barrels. I enlarge the barrels at the ends using a round file. A small sanding drum on a rotary tool can also be used but it is easy to generate heat that way. Cutting with a file keeps things cool. Work uniformly around the circumference, and try the fittings until they slide in without force. Then use a little epoxy to glue them in place.

Tip: The same principles can be applied to any pen, of course, but have proven effective for me in particular with snakewood which also has a tendency to crack.

Section III:
Advanced Projects

11. A Pencil Using a Pentel Mechanism

Arguably the Pentel pencil is the reference standard for mechanical pencils. It is inexpensive, has a reliable mechanism, and is made out of unicolor plastic. We will create a new dress suit for this pencil to make it into a beautiful writing instrument while maintaining the original mechanism. The project requires some unique tooling. I made my own step drill and mandrel, but readymade components are available from John Grounds (The Perfect Connection; see Resources on page 141) for those without metal working capability. Drawing A shows the dimensions of my mandrel. The mandrel (made from drill rod size F) is dimensioned to work in conjunction with the size G drill bit.

In essence we will be turning a wood sleeve. The wall thickness is about .060" and unlike the pen kits we discussed so far this is not supported by an internal brass tube. Of course a brass tube could be incorporated, but I find it unnecessary. However, this means we need to select a wood that has some strength with this thin wall. I chose stabilized black ash burl.

Photo 1 shows the disassembled pencil along with the special tools. There are four parts to the pen: the mechanism (1), the tip (2), the sleeve (3) and the clip (4). Just unscrew the nib on the original pencil to disassemble. We will replace the sleeve and re-use the other parts.

Tools & Materials

- Lathe and standard tooling
- Pentel P205 (or P207 or P209) pencil
- Mandrel and bushings for Pentel pencil from The Perfect Connection
- "G" aircraft drill bit (6" long)
- ¼" to ⁵⁄₃₂" step drill 6" long (or make your own)
- Collet chuck (e.g. Beall collet chuck) with 7 mm collet
- Stabilized wood blank (black ash burl), at least 4.5" long

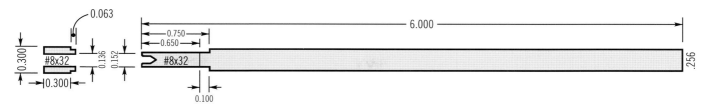

A. Custom mandrel for Pentel

Because the mandrel is very thin on one end, it makes sense to reduce the stress induced during initial roughing while knocking off the corners. So I first turn the blank round, using a scroll chuck with #0 jaws. Of course, you can do it between centers also, or use a disk sander to roughly turn it round.

Note: If you buy a commercial mandrel, the diameters may be slightly different. John Grounds sells a $^{17}/_{64}$" drill bit and matching size "G" mandrel.

Drill with G bit (0.261") to a depth of 4.3". This is the challenge in this project. A mini-lathe with bed extension has enough room

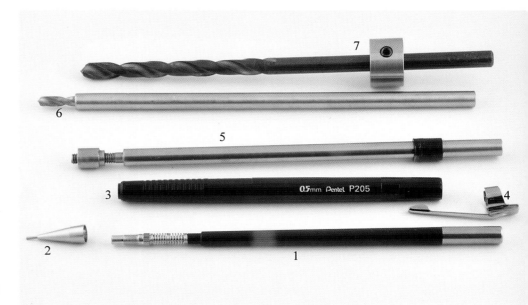

1. Disassembled Pentel pencil with specialized tools.

to drill to this depth. You can also use a drill press. If your drill press does not have a long enough stroke, you may need to use the technique outlined in Chapter 3 to drill in stages. I use a depth stop. A piece of masking tape may also be used. The depth is critical and measured to the tip of the drill bit, not the shoulder. Because the flutes are less than 3" long, withdraw the bit often to avoid loading the flutes with chips. Loaded flutes generate a lot of heat. After drilling about 2", using the lathe ram, you can loosen the tailstock and carefully advance the drill by pushing the whole tailstock directly (Photo 3). Note that if you use a stable material like Corian, you can drill letter F, the same size as the mandrel, because Corian will not warp nor will the hole turn out undersize. Then drill a second, concentric $^5/_{32}$" hole using a step drill. I made my own "step drill" by drilling a $^5/_{32}$" hole; about 1" deep into the center of a piece of ¼" drill rod. I then used epoxy to secure a 1.5" piece of a $^5/_{32}$" drill (item 6 in Photo 1). The original hole was drilled .261" (letter "G").

2. Pre-rounding a blank in a four jaw chuck.

The smaller ¼" rod is chosen so it actually turns freely in the hole since holes in wood are usually smaller than the drill bit. Drill till the rod bottoms out in the first hole. If you are using a commercial step drill, it is best to drill most of the way with a standard drill bit, then switch to the step drill for the last little bit, using a depth stop.

Now cut the blank to exactly 4.45" on the band saw. If you find that the ⁵⁄₃₂" hole does not exit in the center, don't worry about it! Check that the Pentel mechanism fits; it should protrude and show a few threads (Photo 4).

3. After the hole is drilled about 2" deep, use the ram to loosen the tailstock and advance it as a unit.

Put the blank on the mandrel. My mandrel (item 5 in Photo 1) is made from size F drill rod (0.257") and provides a fairly snug fit. If there is a gap at the large end, use a thin brass shim bent around the mandrel to support it. (Photo 5) Add a .340" bushing at the large end and screw on the threaded step bushing at the small end. Tighten the bushing by hand. Now unscrew the bushing about two or three turns and push the blank up against it. This creates a little space so you can tighten the threaded bushing later. Secure the mandrel in the collet chuck eliminating the space just created, and retighten the bushing.

Turn the blank to a .375" diameter using the tool of your choice. The ½" gouge does a good job. Taper the headstock end to the bushing. At the tailstock (tip end) taper to approximately the large diameter of the bushing; it is not terribly critical. Then use a thin parting tool and turn a short tenon (perhaps .040" wide) down to the small diameter of the step bushing. Turn a little radius at the step if you want, or do that while you sand.

4. Test the fit and look for the proper protrusion. A few threads need to be exposed to secure the tip.

5. A brass shim may be needed if the hole is too large.

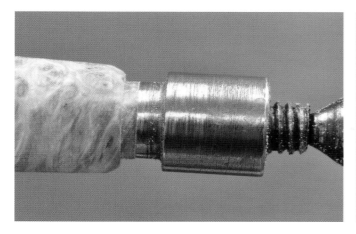

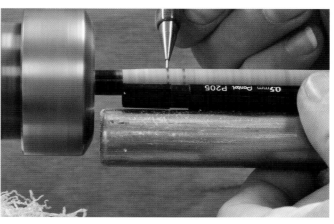

6. Use a thin parting tool to make a short tenon down to the smaller bushing diameter.

7. Use the original barrel to mark the location of the clip recess.

8. A shopmade tool lets you slide the clip onto the pencil without leaving marks.

9. The finished pencil.

Use the original sleeve as a guide to mark the location of the clip recess (Photo 7). Use a parting tool to create a recess for the clip, about .020" deep. Use the finish of your choice. A CA finish is durable and polishes well. After applying CA redefine the clip recess and step at the tip.

Assemble the pen by inserting the mechanism and screwing on the tip. The tip should fit over the short tenon. To put on the clip I made a little jig from a

10 mm brass tube that was a spare tube from a cigar pen kit. I then glued a piece of wood into it and turned a taper. Slide the clip onto the taper and the brass tube, set the brass tube on the pen, and slide the clip forward onto the pen until it seats in the recess.

Sit back and admire your beautiful pencil! Of course, you can customize the shape to your liking. Maybe add little grooves like the original if you want, although I like it the way it is shown here in Photo 9.

12. Laser-cut Ballpoint Pen

Laser-cut pen kits arrived on the scene in 2003. I met Ken Nelsen at the 1st Annual Pen Turners Rendezvous in Provo, Utah. He was full of ideas and later that year introduced the first laser-cut kit. Things sure took off from there, and there are many kits available from all the main pen kit distributors, most produced by Ken. The kit I am using here is a prototype, it demonstrates the basics though it may look a little different when it is released.

The kits are like a three-dimensional inlay on a pen barrel. The pieces are cut out of contrasting woods by a computer-controlled laser. Photo 1 shows the pieces as they come out of the bag. The pieces are assembled on a loose Sierra brass tube, and held together with small rubber bands (Photo 2).The brass tube can be withdrawn at this point.

This kit has a special challenge; the sound hole is a clear window that shows the maker's label inside the guitar. Since this is a reasonably costly kit, and involves a technique I had not tried before, I made a test first, to practice this aspect. I would recommend this before trying this kit for the first time. Photo 1 includes the test piece, a pen blank drilled for a Sierra tube ($^{27}/_{64}$"), with some $^5/_{16}$" holes cut in the side. Make the blank a little longer than the brass tube so you can rescue the tube without shortening it. Ken had suggested epoxy to make a clear window in the

Tools & Materials

- Mini lathe with standard accessories

- Laser-cut guitar pen kit from Kallenshaan Woods

- Sierra or similar ⅜" tube pen kit

- Sierra bushings

- Belt or disk sander with sanding jig for squaring blanks

- Epoxy, CA glue

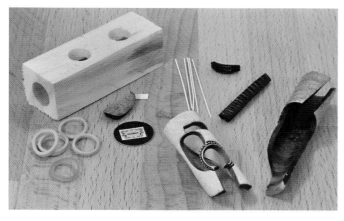

1. Guitar kit parts, with a test blank used to produce a clear window.

2. After assembly on a temporary brass tube, parts are held together by small rubber bands.

3. Some test labels printed on an inkjet are applied to test the windows.

4. The test holes after filling. Epoxy on right, CA on left.

sound hole. I printed a test pattern on a self-adhesive label and applied it to the brass tube, aligned with the holes (Photo 3). I then mixed some 5-minute epoxy and transferred some into one of the holes. I filled the hole to the top. You may find that some air bubbles are evident. You can get rid of these by lightly passing over the hole with the flame from a butane lighter. Photo 4 shows some minor scorching. This is only skin-deep and will be turned away! Allow sufficient time for the epoxy to cure enough to be turned and polished.

> *Tip:* *You can chemically blacken brass tubes. Look for "Liver of Sulphur," available in art supply stores.*

For a CA fill, I tried thin as well as medium CA. One drop at a time, each drop is cured with accelerator. (If you fill the hole to the top you will have to wait a long time for the CA to cure throughout.) Turn the barrel close to the bushings and apply a quick polish/CA finish. Photo 5 shows both test windows. In three attempts I always had some bubbles remaining with CA, so epoxy-fill it is for me. You can rescue the brass tube by turning away the test wood and windows. The actual pen is surprisingly simple to make. I like to paint the brass tube black for these kits. That way, if there are small gaps, you won't see bright brass through the cracks. I use spray paint from the hardware store. Apply the maker's label to the blackened brass tube and slide it into the rubber-banded barrel, carefully aligning it with the sound hole. Remember to angle it to line up with the angled guitar! Fill the sound hole as described above. Insert the white rectangular piece of styrene as saddle into the bridge (non-guitar players, see Photo 6) and use thin white styrene rods to plug the six bridge pins and position markers in the finger board. Push a piece of the rod to the bottom of the hole and cut with a suitable tool such as a razor blade. Apply some thin CA to lock them in place.

Flow thin CA along all of the seams. Enough CA will wick down and adhere all the pieces to the brass tube. I usually follow with medium CA to make sure the seams are filled. Apply accelerator, and trim the ends square. This has to be done on a sander, not a barrel trimmer. If you don't have a belt or disk sander with

a squaring jig (see sidebar, page 23) you could do this freehand and trim the excess material close to the brass tube. Use a shop made squaring sander like the one below to square.

Turn with very sharp tools to the bushings. I use my favorite ½" spindle gouge. When sanding mixed woods you need to be careful not to 'dirty up' the lighter woods. After your last cut with gouge or skew, apply a thin layer of CA to seal the surface. Let it soak in. When it has cured you can sand without fear of transferring dark wood dust into the lighter woods. Apply a CA finish. Assemble per kit instructions for a pen that will delight any guitar aficionado!

5. After polishing it is clear, the epoxy fill works much better.

6. Little pieces of styrene are inserted as bridge pins, fret markers and saddle.

Making a Handy Squaring Tool

A handy squaring tool that uses sandpaper can be made very simply from an old piece of mandrel. It is ideal for working on pre-turned barrels. I use a ¾" diameter by ½" steel cylinder. If you don't have metalworking capability, you can turn a hardwood cylinder. Fit it into a convenient handle. Make sure the front is flat and square and drill a ¼" hole on the lathe which will fit the .246" mandrel. Epoxy the mandrel in. Cut a ¾" square out of self-adhesive sand paper (commonly available as stick-on disks for pad sanders). Use a hole punch to punch a hole into the center and stick it over the exposed mandrel. Use it like a pen mill. It will not replace a pen mill but can do trimming jobs like this and is ideal for anything you may need to do on a finished pen barrel.

A shopmade sanding trimmer.

13. Aluminum Fountain Pen

Aluminum can be worked with woodworking tools quite easily. On a metal lathe, aluminum is worked with tool bits made from high-speed steel (HSS). Most woodworking lathe tools are also made from HSS, so they are certainly capable of cutting aluminum! Aluminum comes in different alloys. The most common alloy is 6061, usually sold as 6061-T6 where the T6 refers to the temper. 6061 is excellent for pens, better than some of the softer alloys you might find in the corner hardware store. 7075 is also very good to use for pens.

You can cut aluminum rod right on your woodworking band saw. The default blade I use is six teeth per inch, ½" wide blade, and it cuts it with ease. It does get warm! Cut just a little longer then the brass tubes; there is no problem with the drill bit exiting the blank in aluminum.

The El Grande cap barrel has a diameter of .590". The starting rod is .625" (⅝"). This means there is not a lot of extra, and the hole needs to be centered well. To assure that, I mark the center on the lathe using a centering drill (Photo 1). A centering drill is a very short drill that is accurately ground to a point. Even if entered slightly off-center, it will pull itself into the center of the rotation. After the center is marked, I move to the drill press. It's easy to find the center to start your drill. The cap barrel requires a ³³⁄₆₄" drill. In wood, that drill usually produces a hole that is too tight, and some vendors offer 13.3 mm drills specifically for that hole. In aluminum, there is no shrinkage, and ³³⁄₆₄" works perfectly. I run the drill press around 1200 RPM (a default setting that my drill

Tools & Materials

- Lathe and standard tooling
- El Grande fountain kit (Berea)
- Bushings for El Grande (Berea)
- Pen mill shim barrels (make your own)
- 5" length of ⅝" aluminum 6061-T6
- ³¹⁄₆₄" and ³³⁄₆₄" drill bits

Note: If you don't want to deal with cutting and drilling rod you can buy some readymade aluminum blanks from HUT Products, but only in a few models.

press is usually set to) and drill at ⅜" first, followed by ³³⁄₆₄" (Photo 2). When you drill aluminum, you get long sharp ribbons that whisk around. They are very sharp! It is best to peck at drilling. When you stop advancing the drill the ribbon is cut so you get shorter pieces. Aluminum chips are nasty. They get into your shoe soles and scratch up your floor, so clean up right away!

Glue in the brass tubes with epoxy. Why use brass tubes at all? They are not necessary but make life easier. It is actually not trivial to drill aluminum and get to a diameter where you can press in the fitting directly. Of course it can be done, ideally finishing with a reamer of the exact diameter.

Square the blanks using a sharp pen mill or sanding jig, using appropriate filler-sleeves. Chuck them up, sharpen your tool, and start turning! The ½" gouge works quite well as long as you take small cuts (Photo 3). Be aware that aluminum will heat up quite a bit when you turn it, so allow occasional cooling time.

Just like with wood, the quality of your final cut will determine what sandpaper to start with. It may be a little coarser than what you are used to. You need to get rid of all tool marks. Work up to 600 grit at least. Then you can switch to automotive wet-or-dry paper and continue, using some oil as lubricant. Honing oil works well. Go up to 1500 or 2000 grit. At any time you can decide this is enough and just give it a pass with 220 grit, running it slowly left to right, for a 'brushed' finish. You should do this after going at least to 600 though, because you often see tool marks appear at finer grits that were not visible before.

Alternatively, you can bring the aluminum to a near mirror shine with various polishing pastes. Automotive supply stores have a variety of polishes. As with other finishes it is important to do a complete job at each stage, before you go to the next finer one. I've used Mother's Mag & Aluminum polish, and Nu-Shine II. I think most of these polishes are for a final oxide removal; they will not remove scratches. I usually run micro-mesh up to 12,000 and think the finish I end up with is better than the wet-or-dry paper route. I list all these options because this is really up to individual experimentation, after the initial sanding to 600.

Press the parts together according to the instructions.

Voila! A beautiful aluminum pen!

1. Center drill the aluminum blanks.

2. Drilling the cap barrel.

3. The ½" gouge works quickly on aluminum.

Tip: For the center band fitting, use a tiny bit of epoxy. The fitting is made from Delrin which does not adhere well to glue, but whatever little grip the epoxy has on it, it is enough to prevent the fitting from getting pulled out by hand.

14. The Versatile Slimline Pen Kit

The slimline kit is the most popular of all pen kits, for a number of reasons. It is also the oldest and least expensive kit available. Therefore, it is very attractive to novice pen turners. At under $2 a kit you don't have to worry too much about making a mistake. However, to make it perfect with straight barrels is actually quite challenging. The wood layer is amongst the thinnest of any kit, and the transition to the metal parts needs to be spot on or you can feel it. Thus the mandrel has to be very straight, and cutting and finishing techniques have to be good. Unfortunately, the quality of these low-priced kits varies. There are small dimensional differences between suppliers. For example, the center band is often very loose on the transmission and moves around creating a step you can feel. So there are some frustrations to overcome! Nonetheless, many people start with this pen. The kit is also available in several finishes. Out of the low-price finishes, I would advise buying the chrome plated version; it is much more durable than similarly priced 24k gold plated kits.

The slimline kit has some features that make it extremely easy to modify and customize. What makes the slimline unique is that the transmission is pressed into the tube. If your tube is short, do not press the transmission in as far. It you use a longer tube, just insert it further! The instructions tell you to insert to a mark on the transmission. Ignore that instruction. Instead, make a length gauge, a block of wood exactly $3^{15}/_{16}$" long. When pressing the transmission in, add this gauge between the jaws of the press (Photo 1). Strictly speaking, this length only works if the assembly press jaws do not have a recess, so you may have to modify it. But once you know the right length for your assembly press, that's it, no matter what the exact length of the pen barrel is.

When assembling slimline pens, you need to be especially careful to keep the parts aligned. Because of the small tube diameter the tip, in particular, likes escaping sideways, leading to a cracked barrel. Some of the assembly jigs sold by the kit suppliers have special inserts to alleviate this problem. I particularly

1. A simple gauge for assembling slimline pens.

like the Pen-Ultimate assembly jig sold by Craft Supplies USA that lets you assemble slimline (and other) pens using your lathe. It does an excellent job keeping components aligned (Photo 2).

There are several commercial variations of the slimline kit on the market. One of the first of these was the Father Sing kit, which uses a longer front tube and has a fatter center band. Some variations named 'Comfort' or 'Softgrip' add a rubber grip section which you may or may not use. These also beef up the center band slightly to give the pen a pleasing curve. Craft Supplies has a double-bead version of the slimline that makes it more forgiving in diameter. There is a 'Presidential Pen Kit' that uses a very different clip. Berea has a "Streamline

2. An on-the-lathe assembly jig.

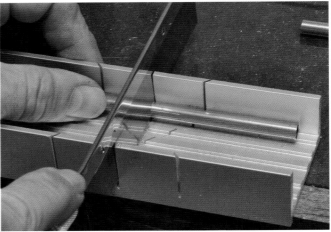

3. An X-acto miter box and saw can be used to cut brass tubes without damage.

4. A wood block with a hole for the brass tube prevents the tube from collapsing when sawn on the band saw.

Slimline" that uses a yet another clip style and a larger diameter triple-bead center band. These are just a few. Often retail stores give new names to the same kit to differentiate them. The whole genre is referred to as "7 mm pens" because they are based on 7 mm diameter brass tubes, and all use the same twist mechanism and Cross-style refill. Within the 7 mm system you can mix and match, although platings seem to vary from batch to batch. Dimensions have quite a range so it's always a good idea to measure components. The interchangeability lets you buy longer brass tubes as spares for other kits and you can use them in your creations.

In the next few chapters I will show you some designs based on the slimline kit. If you start with slimline kits to get the basic components, you may want to get some long 7 mm brass tubes that you can cut to size yourself. They are available in 10" lengths, even plated or pre-painted to make them easier to use in translucent acrylic pens. You can cut brass tubes using a scroll saw, or a small miter box and fine-tooth saw such as X-acto used by railroad modelers to cut tracks (Photo 3). I find a tiny chop saw, sold by Harbor Freight or Penn State Industries, quite useful for this task. It is actually the only task this saw does well in the pen shop. If you try to cut a brass tube on a band saw it will collapse. If that is your only tool option, drill a 7 mm hole into a block of wood and insert the tube. Cut through the tube but don't exit the wood so you can re-use the jig. Being trapped in a hole the tube can't distort and will not collapse (Photo 4).

Some excellent examples of pens based on the 7 mm kits can be found on the web at:

http://penmakersguild.com/provo03/pp03/pendisplay03names.htm

http://penmakersguild.com/provo04/pp04/pendisplay04names.htm

http://penmakersguild.com/provo05/pp05/pendisplay05names.htm

http://penmakersguild.com/provo06/pp06/pendisplay06names.htm

The finished pen with an integrated center band.

15. Classic Slimline Pen Customizations

You can make your own center bands for slimline kits, in several ways. First, let's make some loose center bands that fit the transmission with no play. You can make such centerbands from plastic sheet material of a suitable thickness around ¼". Here I take a pen blank and rip a strip of ¼" thickness on the band saw, ending up with a strip ¼" x ¾" x 5".

Smooth the sawn surface on some sandpaper. Lay the sandpaper on a flat surface and rub the strip back and forth. Drill "D" (.246") holes. Avoid chipout where the drill bit exits by clamping down the workpiece and drilling into a wasteboard. Cut small rectangles on the band saw; high accuracy is not required. Stack the squares on the mandrel; use some bushings to fill the empty space on a fixed mandrel (Photo 2). Turn them to the desired diameter, and polish using your preferred plastic polishing method. I use micro-mesh. If you want to make a straight replacement for the stock center band, make the diameter .331". Photo 3 shows a completed pen with such a center band. With a simple addition, this pen, made from relatively plain looking Osage orange wood, takes on a custom look!

You can turn a single center band with a fancy shape in a similar way. The end offcuts from pen blanks are a great starting material. Cut a block of the desired thickness and drill with a "D" bit. Use filler blocks (shim barrels you made for the pen mill come in handy!) and/or spare

Tools & Materials

- Mini-lathe and standard tooling
- Slimline ('7 mm') kits
- "D" (.246") drill bit
- ⁹⁄₃₂" drill bit or "J"
- Wood pen blank
- Acrylic pen blank, or plastic sheet material, ⅛"–¼" thick
- Pen blank cut-offs

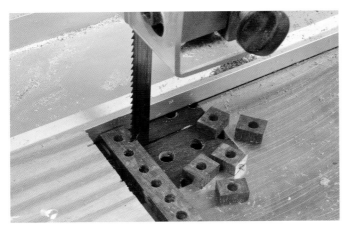

1. Drill holes in a strip of material and use the band saw to separate the material into squares.

2. The blanks stacked on the mandrel.

3. A pen using a custom bushing.

4. Use filler pieces to mount a single center band on a mandrel.

bushings on the mandrel to lock the block in place with the mandrel nut (Photo 4). Such a shaped center band looks best with a shaped pen. You can be as fanciful and creative as you want. With the slimline, and your own center band, the design of the pen center is entirely up to you!

There is no reason to make a loose center band. We can integrate it into one of the barrels. In the next pen we'll add the center band to the upper barrel. To allow the pen to still function properly we need to increase the length of one of the brass tubes by the width of the stock center band which we eliminated. For visual balance we'll put the extra length on the lower body, using a 2¼" to 2⅜" tube there. You can cut a tube from long stock or get a replacement tube meant for a 7 mm round-top (a.k.a. Euro) pen. At the same time we'll also increase the diameter of the upper barrel a bit, creating a small step in the center. The reason for this is visual appearance, but also fault tolerance. If the turning is slightly off-center, this shows up when the pen is twisted to advance the refill

and is one of the reasons the slimline, as designed, is actually not trivial for a novice. A slight deliberate step hides such a defect effectively.

I used olive for this pen. Prepare the blanks the standard way. Cut your wood about ⅜" longer than the brass tube. Drill down the center with a 9⁄32" or "J" drill stopping just before the bit exits. Cut the blanks to the length of the brass tubes, opening the end. Glue in the brass tubes using epoxy. Square the ends using a pen mill or sanding jig. Mount the blanks on the mandrel using slimline bushings. This is all standard procedure so far.

Turn the barrels round but not to the bushings yet. Since we will have to take a blank off the mandrel

> *Tip:* To avoid melting/smearing acrylics on the band saw, spray the blade (while it is running) under the table with a cooking spray such as Pam.

5. A pen using a custom shaped bushing.

6. Use a parting tool to cut a tenon down to the brass tube for an integrated center band.

7. Glue on a slice of wood using CA.

8. With the lathe on high speed, use some wire to burn decorative marks.

and remount, we want to leave final turning until the blanks can stay on through the rest of the process. About 0.4" is right for now. Create space for the center band on the upper barrel by turning down to the brass tube using a parting tool. Make the width about ¼" (Photo 6). Now we will be adding a contrasting wood center band. By doing this on the pen barrel rather than just gluing two pieces of wood together at the start, we can be sure that the wood joint is perfectly true with the pen. It is amazing how little such a junction has to be off square to be noticeable!

Take a suitable contrasting offcut, a little longer than the brass tube you exposed, and drill it ⁹⁄₃₂" or "J". Sand one face flat. You can do this freehand on the belt sander or on a flat table. It is not necessary to use a barrel trimmer. Remove the shorter, upper barrel, from the mandrel and test-fit the piece. The smooth side is located against the existing wood. It should be in full contact with no gaps. Use thick CA on the exposed brass tube to glue the center band slice on. A shot of accelerator sets the CA quickly. Now use your

barrel trimmer or sanding jig to trim the excess back to the brass tube. Remount on the mandrel (Photo 7) and turn the pen to shape. Note that I positioned the center band at the tailstock. Usually mandrels run truer there than in the middle. Turn the lower barrel to your liking, the tip end should be to the .331" bushing. The center band is about .375" (use calipers or go by look and feel, comparing the step to the bushing), the clip end is to the bushing .331". I think the step looks better if rounded over slightly. You can dress up the center band in several ways. One easy way is a burn mark generated with a piece of piano wire or a 'wire burner' which is also piano wire with some very convenient handles. Cut a small groove using the long point of a skew or something like a pyramid tool. Even a parting tool presented at 45° can cut enough of a groove for the wire to run in. Turn the lathe to high speed and stretch the wire over the groove till you see a little smoke coming off (Photo 8).

Sand, polish, finish and assemble using the length gauge. What a beauty!

16. Sweetheart Pen

In this chapter we'll advance the design a little further. By giving the body more shape, improving the step in the center, and adding a rounded, turned finial we can make a custom pen very much like a "Euro" design. In addition, we'll add a special center band for a total custom look. This shows you what you can do with this kit that does not restrict you in center diameter and tube length. I am packing a number of advanced elements into this pen. It may seem a little complex, but you can use the elements in any combination that suits you to create your own personal custom design.

The center bands I will use here are prepared beforehand. Drill half a pen blank of African blackwood with a ⁹⁄₃₂" or "J" drill and turn to .460". You can do this on the pen mandrel, using a loose brass tube. I drew a heart pattern and sent it to my laser engraver to cut six heart shaped pockets on a perimeter, not quite breaking through to the drilled hole. Repeat the pattern on the barrel, on a .28" pitch. This lets me cut ¼" center bands with my thin parting tool (see page 4) which has a .03" kerf (Photo 1). Little markers between the individual bands are a guide for

Tools & Materials

- Lathe and standard tooling
- Collet chuck or drill chuck with draw bar
- Pyramid tool
- Slimline kit
- Slimline bushings
- Finial adapter from 7 mm Euro kit (available as replacement part)
- Cap stud mandrel (Craft Supplies USA)
- Cap studs (Craft Supplies USA)
- Pink ivory pen blank
- African blackwood pen blank, optional
- Crushed turquoise or similar
- Thin ivory slab or similar (optional)
- M5 x 0.8 metric bottoming tap (e.g. Enco part number 325-5171)
- ⅜" counterbore with ¼" pilot (e.g. Enco part number 368-1024 with 368-3116)

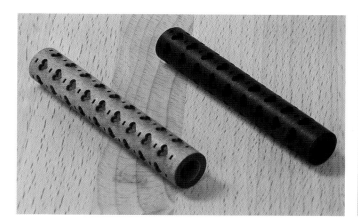

1. A series of laser-cut center bands.

2. The recess for a clip is cut using a pen mill modified on a grinder.

3. The clip recess cut with the modified pen mill.

4. A piece of mammoth ivory, flattened on one side, is glued on as an accent.

cutting but this can also be judged by eye. By ganging the center bands in that way the laser operation becomes more efficient and cost effective.

Start by preparing the pink ivory barrels. Cut slightly long, drill a little short of breaking through, cut to length, and glue in the brass tubes. This pen features a hidden clip, and now is a good time to cut the recess for it because the blank is easy to hold. I ground notches into a small pen mill head so it will cut .340" diameter (Photo 2). You can do this freehand on a grinder, or with a handheld Dremel tool and a cutoff disk or stone. Proceed slowly when you do this. Try to take even amounts off each cutting edge, and test often. It is actually easier than it sounds! By limiting the depth of what you cut away you generate a convenient depth stop. The depth of the pocket you want to cut is a little more than the thickness of the clip ring, roughly .030".

Mount the blanks on the lathe with 7 mm bushings and turn to about 0.5" diameter. The bushing at the clip end will contact inside the clip pocket we cut earlier. Cut a ¼" wide tenon down to the brass tube, using the parting tool. I like adding an extra accent here, a thin piece of ivory drilled with the ⁹⁄₃₂" bit. You can obtain ivory removed from piano keys. Folks that rebuild pianos will often have some for sale. I bought a pound of mammoth ivory scraps once that has yielded many accents. With an irregular shape, flatten one side on sand paper, glue that side on, then use your parting tool to turn a flat face to glue the center band against. I use CA here. A shot of accelerator lets you continue right away.

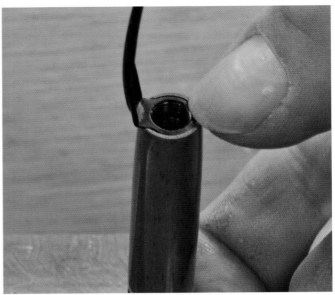

5. A piloted counterbore can be used to cut a recess into the center band to create an overlap on the lower barrel.

7. Test-fitting the clip.

6. Flowing CA into the stone, using a micro-tip.

Glue on the center band with CA. We want to overlap the center band slightly over the lower barrel so there is no visible gap where the pen halves come together. You can make a recess cutter similar to the one used for the clip recess, but I chose to buy a commercial ⅜" counterbore with ¼" pilot (Photo 5). The shaft has to be reduced slightly to fit into the brass tube. This can be done easily by removing the pilot and holding it in the collet chuck, and using a file. The depth of the

recess you cut is not critical. About .02" is sufficient. You don't want to be near the laser cut pockets.

Use calipers to turn to the following dimensions: lower tube .331" at the tip (match the tip of your particular hardware!), .370"–.372" at the center. The reason for the .370" is that the barrel will fit into a ⅜" recess of the center band. The upper barrel is turned to just cut into the center band, so about .455". This leaves a .040" rim overlapping the lower barrel, and is the reason we started the center band barrels with .460" diameter. The clip end is turned to .380". Since we made the recess cutter .340" diameter, that leaves a .020" rim which is adequate. A little more will work also, if you make it too fat, the clip bend will sit very close to the barrel and look a little odd.

Now we can fill the center band pockets. I like using crushed turquoise stone. Fill one pocket at a time with stone. Try to get the stone level, a little overfill will not hurt and will be removed when you finish turn. Avoid gaps where you can see to the bottom of the laser cut pocket. Use a micro-tip on a bottle of thin CA to carefully flow some CA into the stone until it looks soaked. The micro-tip helps control the flow. If you use a big drop, it may wash the stone out of the pocket, and if the CA solidifies in the pocket without stone, you'll have to turn the centerband off with the parting tool and use another.

Turn off any stone that landed on the surface. If you overfilled a lot, a carbide-tipped tool comes in handy because this stone is rather hard! Once all the stone is off the surface you can add more medium CA until all the pockets are filled. Then level the surface again and blend it into the pen. Round over the center band edge for a nice look. Sand, polish and finish with your favorite finish. I use CA. Be careful not to round over the clip end! If you have the sandpaper pen mill (Photo 4) you can use it to resquare the clip end and give it a sharp edge but keep an eye on the depth of the pocket.

Use either a needle file, or a small wheel on a Dremel, to cut a channel for the clip. Because of the way the clip is bent sometimes it's difficult to test the fit in the proper position. So, flip it over to test the channel fit (Photo 7). The clip ring should fit completely into the pocket, and the clip should fit the channel snugly. Then press in a finial adapter from a 7 mm Euro, tapered end first. You can leave it flush with the rim of the barrel to help center the clip and give it extra strength, but you need to make sure the clip can slide over it. Unfortunately, there is a fair amount of dimensional variation in slimline hardware.

All we have left to do now is make the custom finial. I arrived at the method I present here after many attempts that had moderate success; this one works nearly 100%. It makes sense to prepare several finials at a time. Cut ⅜" thick slices off a suitable pen blank. I used African blackwood here. Flatten one side by rubbing on sandpaper on a flat surface. Mark a corner so you can repeatedly mount it in the drill vise. Mount it in the drill vise so the flattened side is up and flush with the jaws—this gives a consistent reference surface. Drill to a depth of 3/16" using a 9/64" drill bit. A twist drill works best here, with a pilot

8. Pre-drilling the finial.

9. The drill bit guides the tap to keep it vertical.

> *Tip:* *It is important that the tapped hole be square to the flat surface. To assure that I use the 9/64" drill to guide the tap wrench. The tap wrench has a hole in the end that fits that drill bit (Photo 8). If the tap bottoms out it will destroy the thread. To avoid that, count the number of turns. Four turns work for me.*

10. The easiest way to shape the finial is using a pyramid-point tool. Note the .380" diameter sizing bushing that can be slid up against the finial.

point or brad point you risk exposing the smaller hole at the end when you turn the finial (Photo 7). Use an M5 x 0.8 metric bottoming drill in a tap wrench to cut a thread in the finial. Glue a cap stud into the cut thread.

Mount the stud mandrel in a collet or drill chuck. I add a small sizing ring I made with diameter .380". You can make it out of anything stable such as metal, plastic, or Corian because you slide it away during turning. Thread the blank onto the cap stud and turn it to a diameter just over .380", using the sizing ring as reference. An experienced turner will use the spindle gouge or skew to give the finial the right shape. For a less experienced turner, or even a relative novice, I would suggest the pyramid tool. Swing it in a horizontal arc while keeping the bevel rubbing and you will easily generate the perfect finial shape (Photo 9). It is really easy to keep the bevel rubbing because the tool is round. The diameter and curvature needs to match the cap you turned. You can take the finial off and try it on the pen.

Tip: *If you don't have a collet chuck you can use a drill chuck with a threaded MT2 arbor to hold the stud mandrel. Use a piece of all thread, a wooden centering plug, washer and nut to hold the chuck in the headstock so it will not come out during turning. It is not held captive like a pen mandrel for example!*

Now sand, polish and apply your finish, preserving a sharp corner against the pen. Apply a tiny amount of epoxy to the inside of the clip recess with a toothpick, and lock the clip in place with the finial. Press the tip into the small diameter end of the lower barrel, and the transmission into the other end, using the assembly gauge. Slide the upper barrel on and give it to your sweetheart!

17.
Desk Pen

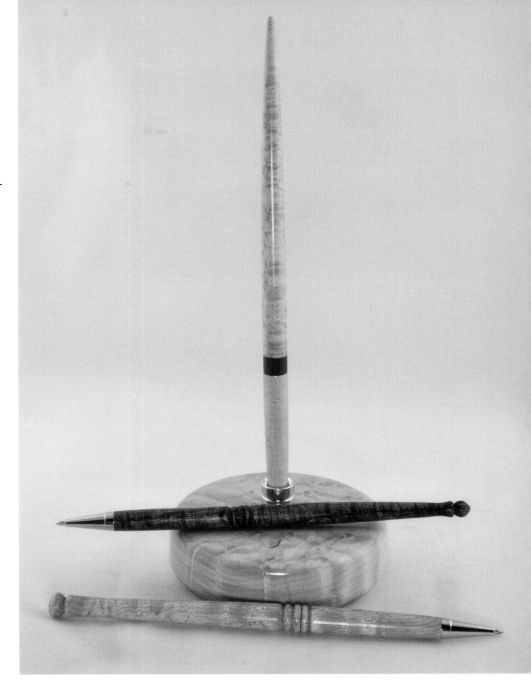

Although you can buy desk pen kits, they can also be made from a regular slimline kit. My method is a little different from the instructions that come with the kits, and I think easier.

The front half of a desk pen is a standard 7 mm barrel. The rear section is longer and cannot be turned on a mandrel; it has a blind hole. Such closed end pens are discussed in Chapter 24 in more detail. The key to my method is a pen mandrel. While a new mandrel shaft is not expensive, you can also use a discarded pen mandrel. It does not matter if it is a little bent or the tailstock end is a little deformed. Grind three flats on it as shown in Photo 1. This can easily be done freehand. The depth of the flats should be a little more than the depth of the threads. Put a slight taper on the last few threads, just like on a tap. The driving end of the shaft is also ground so you can use an adjustable wrench on it. (Photo 2) Remove any burrs with a stone and make sure a 7 mm brass tube slides on easily from either end.

I chose birdseye maple for this pen. Not just because it is beautiful, but also because, like a burl, it does not have a grain structure that might be difficult to match. Six-inch long pen blanks (to make a 7" desk pen) are a little hard to come by unless you cut your own. If you need to combine wood from two blanks, a wood like birdseye maple, or a burl, is a good choice.

I make the closed end upper barrel first and then match the lower barrel to it. Decide on the length you want. For a 7" long pen you need a little

Tools & Materials

- Lathe and standard tooling
- Collet chuck (preferred), or drill chuck with draw bar
- Slimline kit
- Pen mandrel shaft, can be a used (discarded) mandrel
- $\frac{9}{32}$" or "J" drill bit
- $\frac{7}{32}$" drill bit
- One pen blank, 6" long

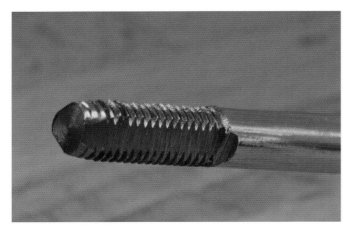

1. Three flats ground on an old pen mandrel turn it into a tap and effective mandrel for desk pens.

2. The other end of the mandrel is ground to accept a wrench.

3. With the tip of the drill bit even with the top of the blank, use the brass tube to set the depth of the hole a little longer than the tube.

over 2" for the front part and about 4" for the upper barrel. Cut the blank, and center drill with ⁹⁄₃₂" to a depth about ¼" longer than the brass tube. The easiest way to set the depth is to advance the drill until it is even with the top of the blank. Then set the brass tube next to the depth gauge rod and bring the stop nut to about ¼" above the tube (Photo 3) Without disturbing the blank, change the drill bit to ⁷⁄₃₂" and drill another ½" to ¾" beyond the first hole.

Remove the blank from the drill vise. Use epoxy to glue in one of the brass tubes. Scuff up the brass tube with some sandpaper. Coat the outside of the tube with epoxy and insert it into the upper blank, the end flush with the end of the wood. There is no need to square the ends of the blank. After the epoxy has cured, insert the converted mandrel into the brass tube. You may find a little epoxy blocking the end of the tube, just push past it. Use an adjustable wrench to screw the mandrel into the secondary (⁷⁄₃₂") hole until it becomes difficult to turn.

Add a 7 mm bushing to the mandrel. If you plan on using a CA finish, make sure the bushing is waxed to prevent CA from sticking. Mount the mandrel in the collet chuck leaving no gap. Bring the tailstock and live center up against the end of the blank and advance the center into the wood. Turn the blank round. When you are down to roughly ½", add an integral center band by cutting a tenon of the desired width down to the brass tube and adding a contrasting wood. This operation is described in Chapter 15. The mandrel stays in the wood, the center band wood is slipped on from the driver end. You can not square the center band at this point because the mandrel is there. We will square up later.

Turn the body to the desired shape. You don't need to turn all the way to the bushing. I turn to .390" here. At the tailstock, leave a small wedge for the live center. Be careful working here. It is a good idea to stabilize the turning with your finger behind the wood when it becomes really thin (Photo 5). Remove the bushing and, using the long point of the skew, square the end of the center band (Photo 6).

4. An integral center band is added.

5. When the wood gets very thin, support it with your finger behind the chisel.

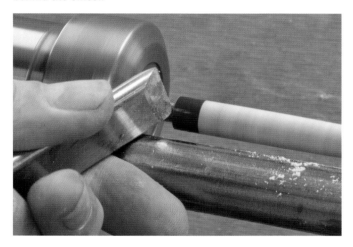

6. Square the center band with the long point of the skew.

Since the entire heavy turning is done by now, you may not need the bushing any more. Its purpose was just to prevent the mandrel from creeping into the collet. Whittle the point at the live center down to almost nothing but leave it attached. Sand, polish and finish. I use my favorite CA finish here. When you sand or polish, always have a supporting finger across from sandpaper, or polishing pad, to avoid breaking the little point. Almost certainly your barrel will not spin on axis if the live center is not there.

Now you can whittle some more at the tip. Move the tailstock away and break off the little cone. I tend to just sand the very end a little with 600 paper and don't bother with CA finish. A little wax is all the tiny area gets.

The front barrel is completely standard fare. Turn one end to the bushing (.331") and the other to the center band diameter; .390" for this pen.

A desk pen does not need a retractable nib. You can leave the transmission operational, but you can also disable it. To do that, twist the transmission to advance it. Using a micro-tip, flow a little bit of thin CA into the mechanism. Try to avoid getting it on the threads or you won't be able to screw in the refill. Hit it with accelerator and allow the CA to cure. Press tip and transmission into the front barrel, and push on the upper barrel. Turn a suitable base with a 'funnel', or construct a fancy desk set.

18. Closed End Pen

The challenge in making a closed end pen is one of work holding. In the previous chapter we made a 7 mm desk pen, and that same technique can be expanded to larger pens. I'll also discuss some other techniques to hold a closed end pen. In this project we move partially away from kit components, keeping some parts that are harder to make without metal working equipment. The main body finial is replaced by the closed body. For the center band, we will substitute a sterling silver ring. The stock cap finial is replaced with a turned wooden one.

In searching the web for sterling silver rings, I found that not all ring sizes are easily available. US size four is on the large side for a pen, nominally .586", but is a size easily found. After I ordered some size four rings I was surprised that none of them exactly fit the size specification, most were around .610". I chose the El Toro kit based on the ring dimensions. Photo 1 shows the parts for this ring.

Tools & Materials

- Lathe and standard tooling
- 4-jaw chuck with spigot jaws
- El Toro pen kit (www.arizonasilhouette.com, item BHW-512)
- El Presidente brass tube (www.arizonasilhouette. com, item BHWT-526)
- Bushings for El Presidente
- Schmidt conversion pump
- $^{35}/_{64}$" drill bit, $^{31}/_{64}$" drill bit, "N" drill bit (or other bit around .300")
- Expansion mandrel for El Presidente pen (optional, www.arizonasilhouette.com, item 1918)
- Collet chuck (preferred) or Jacobs-chuck with draw bar
- 1½ or 2 pen blanks (Bethlehem olive wood)
- Sterling Silver Ring, size 4

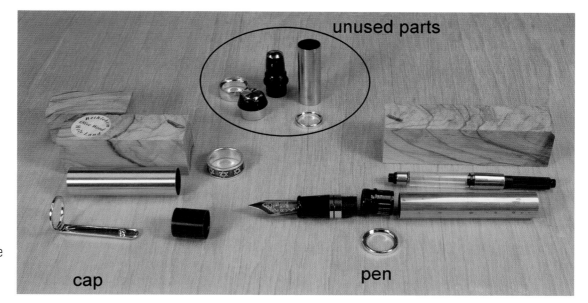

unused parts

cap   pen

1. Several parts from the El Toro kit are not used. A longer brass tube and a sterling ring are added.

The sterling ring should fit over the larger of the two trim rings that come with the kit, the one intended for the rear of the main body. If you find a sterling ring that is closer to the smaller of the trim rings of course you could use that one. It is possible to expand the ring a little by driving a gently tapered steel round into it (see Photo 2). Such a tool can easily be turned on a metal lathe from a piece of steel scrap. A commercial tool is also available, basically a longer tapered piece of steel that you drive the ring on to.

The El Toro uses a short, main body tube. For a full-size pen that can accommodate a spare cartridge or full-size conversion pump, substitute a replacement tube from the El Presidente kit which is the rollerball version. Naturally the whole pen can also be made as a rollerball.

Inside the pen body there should be room for a conversion pump. A Schmidt conversion pump is a little longer than the standard conversion pump so it should be used for size. The Schmidt pump is available from Berea Hardwoods. Dry assemble the parts and take a measurement. (Photo 3). For this pen the required drill depth is 2.75".

Thus for the main body you need a 3" long blank. This allows for a fairly minimal ¼" space to terminate the main barrel. The cap requires 1.97", so a standard pen blank can be used to make both barrels. The cap finial requires about 1.5" of matching wood. It's a good idea to have an extra 1.5" around just in case something goes wrong. I used Bethlehem olive wood here, one of my favorite woods for expressive grain.

2. A wood block and a piece of steel with a slight taper can be used to slightly enlarge a ring.

3. The section, conversion pump, and trim ring are pre-assembled to get the required measurement of the internal length of the main body.

A. A cross section of the pen body.

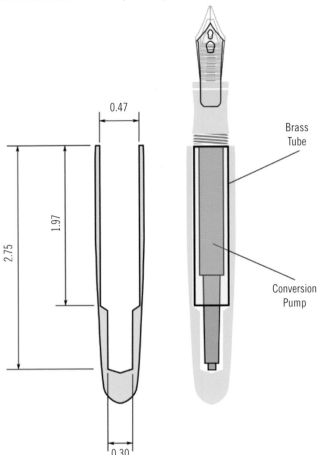

Brass
Tube

Conversion
Pump

0.47

1.97

2.75

0.30

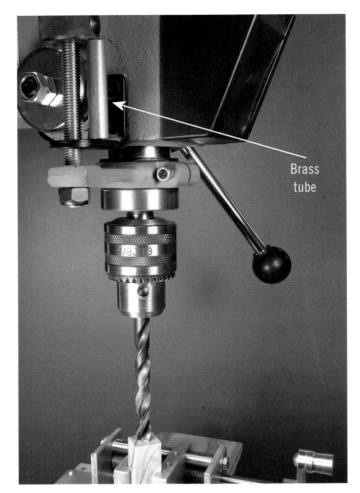

Brass
tube

4. On a drill press with a rod-style depth stop, the brass tube can be used to set the depth of the first hole.

For the main body, drill exactly to the length of the brass tube, using a ³¹⁄₆₄" drill bit. If you have a drill press with a rod type depth stop, you can use the brass tube directly to set the depth. Start to drill until the corner of the cutting edge is even with the top of the blank, lock the quill, and set the depth to the brass tube (Photo 4). After drilling the first hole, without removing the blank from the vise, switch to a size N bit (or ¹⁵⁄₆₄" if you use the mandrel-tap method). Again lock the quill with the bit even with the top of the blanks, set the depth stop to 2.75", and drill to that depth. Drawing A shows a cross-section. Check that the dry assembled front assembly, with conversion pump installed, can be completely inserted into the blank (Photo 5). There should be no gap between wood and trim ring. If necessary drill the smaller hole a little deeper to get a fit. Glue in the brass tube with epoxy, square the face of the blank using a pen mill with appropriate shim barrel,

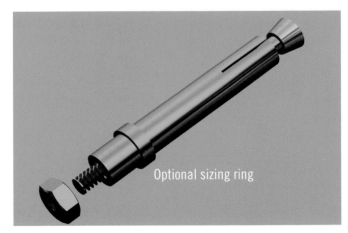

Optional sizing ring

B. An expansion mandrel works by pulling a taper into a slotted end.

5. Test the depth of the main body bore with the assembled section, trim ring, and conversion pump.

6. Mandrel options for closed end pens. From the left: commercial expansion mandrel, a shopmade expansion mandrel, a universal mandrel tap, and a pin chuck.

7. Be mindful of the end of the internal brass tube and use calipers to be certain there is sufficient wall thickness at that weak spot.

8. A pyramid tool makes it easy to round over the end of the barrel.

and deburr it. With a closed end pen, the sanding jig cannot be used. Remove as little material as possible!

For this pen we will use an expansion mandrel. Expansion mandrels are specialized. One mandrel fits exactly one size brass tube. Some alternatives are the mandrel tap, which is universal but less rigid, and a pin chuck that is also dedicated to one brass tube but inexpensive and can be shopmade with just a file. Of course you need access to an appropriately sized piece of steel rod. See the sidebars on these. The expansion mandrel comes with a sizing ring, but because we are using the larger trim ring that is usually at the other end of the body we will not use it here. Photo 6 shows several mandrel options. Drawing B illustrates the operation of the expansion mandrel. A wedge is pulled into the split end of the mandrel by tightening the nut.

Mount the body blank on the expansion mandrel. Slide the barrel on and, using two wrenches, tighten the nut just enough to prevent it from turning. If you make it too tight you may crack the wood. Mount the mandrel in a collet. You can support the end with the tailstock but then you have to remove the dimple left by the live center. I prefer to go easy and turn without outboard support. Turn the headstock end to the diameter of the trim ring, 0.610", using calipers to check your work.

You need to mark the end of the internal brass tube and make sure you leave sufficient wood at that spot for strength. I like to leave around .040" wall thickness. Since the wood was drilled $^{31}/_{64}$" (0.484") the diameter at that point should be around .560". Use a spare brass tube to find the end of the internal brass tube (Photo 7). You can turn any shape you want. I

Using the Mandrel Tap

An old mandrel can be used for closed end pens, similar to what was shown in Chapter 17 for the desk pen. Grind 3 flats onto the threads of a mandrel as illustrated in Drawing C. Instead of drilling a size "N" (.302") hole in the end of the body, drill 7/32". Slide the bushing for the other (open) end onto the mandrel, as illustrated in Drawing D. This is a simple, universal jig. The only disadvantage is that the mandrel is considerably thinner so extra care needs to be taken turning. You may want to knock off the corners of the blank on a belt sander before turning. Also, a "B" mandrel shaft can be used which is 40% stiffer than an "A" mandrel. You can open bushings that are only available for the smaller "A" mandrel, using a "K" drill bit followed by a "L" chucking reamer while holding the bushing in the collet chuck.

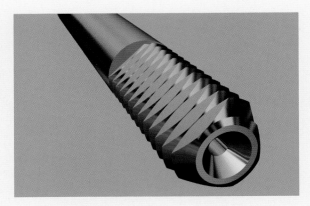

C. Some flats filed into a pen mandrel thread make an easy tap mandrel that can be used for closed end pens.

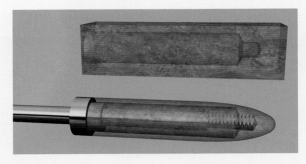

D. In use, a standard bushing supports the open end of the barrel.

tend to favor a classic, slightly tapered, rounded over shape. The simplest, most forgiving way to round the end is by using a diamond point tool. You can swing the tool through the arc without having to reposition the tool rest (Photo 8). A spindle gouge or skew can also be used.

Check the body over carefully for any cracks that may need to be filled. Olivewood can have internal cracks that are brought to the surface by turning. Sand with appropriate grits to 400. With the lathe running on slow, rub some thin CA into the grain as a grain filler, using the same 400 grit sandpaper. The dust that's still on the sandpaper, mixed with the thin CA, makes a slurry that fills tiny cracks and open grain. A shot of accelerator sets the CA quickly. Sand this first application back down to bare wood with 400 grit paper to produce a hard, smooth surface that is an excellent base for the finish. Spread medium CA with your finger covered with a polybag, and hit it with accelerator. Repeat one or two more times. Pay particular attention to the end of the body. Make

sure you have sufficient CA there. Centrifugal force tends to starve this area, and it is very easy to sand/polish through the CA on the curvature. Smooth the surface, scraping with a skew laid flat on the tool rest. Look for about 75% of the shiny surface to disappear. The surface should have a uniform, dull appearance. Now switch back to 400-grit paper again and sand until *all* shiny spots have disappeared. End with length-wise strokes until you see no rings. Now run through micro-mesh 1500, 1800, 2400, 3200 and 4000. Move to the Tripoli polishing wheel followed by white diamond for a high luster. The last step is to square up the shoulder that the trim ring sits against, using a parting tool. This completes the pen body.

The pen can now be assembled. Use extra care because the clamping force is applied directly on the wood, not a metal fitting. I use a leather cover over the anvil of my press. Make sure there is no burr on the brass tube, nor any glue inside that may interfere with the press fit. Screw the grip section into the center coupling and push it on by hand, making

9. Assemble with care, excessive pressure can ruin the finish at the end of the barrel.

10. Sanding the fitting will allow it to slip into the brass tube and be glued in place.

sure the nib is aligned with the best side of the pen. Carefully remove the grip section without disturbing the center coupling and press the fitting home (Photo 9). It is much better to have the fitting loose in the brass tube and use a little epoxy than to have to apply excessive force and risk damage to the pen. You can file the inside of the brass tube, but because of the closed end it's a little awkward. Another method is to grip the fitting in the collet chuck on the threads and use a file or sandpaper to reduce the diameter of the part that slides into the barrel (Photo 10).

Making a Pin Chuck

A pin chuck is a very simple device to hold a pen barrel. It is something that can be made quite easily. It consists of a metal rod that fits snugly inside the brass tube, and a loose pin that acts as an internal cam, sitting on a flat spot of the larger rod. Drawing E illustrates the arrangement. Like the expansion mandrel, it is a specialized chuck working for exactly one size brass tube. Obtain a steel rod that is the right diameter, or slightly larger, for the brass tube to slide on. Many sizes are available as 'drill rod' in the US from machineshop supply houses like Enco, McMaster Carr, MSC Supply, and others. For the El Toro main body, the inside diameter of the brass tube measures .449". This is not a common size, the next size up I can find is $^{29}/_{64}$" (= .453"). This will have to be reduced with a file or sandpaper to .449" for a slip fit of the brass tube. The length should be around 4". A suitable pin can be cut from a nail. Look for a nail around $^{1}/_{8}$" diameter, and cut a ¾" section. File a flat into the rod, a little longer than your pin, and just deep enough so that the brass tube will *just* slide over it. When you apply a twist the brass tube will lock in place. Accuracy counts; a sloppy fit will not lock. But a machineshop is not necessary.

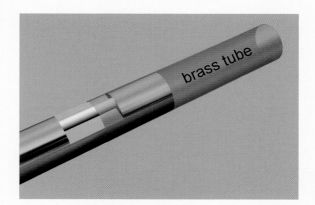

E. A pin chuck in use.

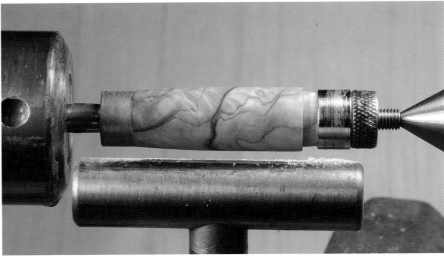

11. Sand one side of the silver ring flat so that it will fit flush.

12. Cut a tenon for the silver ring.

Cut the blank for the cap ⅜" longer than the brass tube. Drill with the ³⁵⁄₆₄" drill bit without letting the drill exit, then cut to the length of the brass tube on the band saw. Use epoxy to glue in the brass tube. Square the ends of the blank using a pen mill or a belt sander and appropriate shim barrel. Use the bushings on a standard mandrel. The clip end of the barrel is turned to the bushing. The center band end needs to be turned to the diameter of the sterling ring.

The ring will sit on a tenon. To meet the square shoulder without a gap, the face of the ring can be sanded carefully on a flat surface (Photo 11). The width of the tenon should be a little less than the width of the ring. The ring will then protrude slightly beyond the wood and overlap the trim ring on the pen body when the pen is closed.

Start by turning a barrel to the measured ring diameter. Cut the tenon to size for a slip fit, using your calipers. Leave the tenon just a little short so you can do a final squaring cut later, after finishing. Now create a gentle curve to the clip end bushing. Sand and finish the same as the pen, making sure to preserve the shoulder. Photo 12 shows the cap barrel with the tenon cut.

For the wood finial, grab the 1.5" long cutoff in a scroll chuck with spigot jaws. We need a ⅜" long tenon to insert into the cap brass tube plus a ½" waste piece for holding the finial after it is reversed.

Make the tenon ⅞" long and of a diameter to just fit inside the brass tube. Use the cap to size it. Drill a ⅜" diameter hole, ⅞" deep to make some room for the pen nib. (Photo 13).

Switch back to the Beall chuck with an appropriate collet and hold the finial reversed. Shape it, using calipers for size. See Photo 14. Try to match the slope of the cap tube for a continuous look, sand and finish. Again, end with a squaring cut at the shoulder. Then part off the ½" waste piece leaving a ⅜" section to glue into the tube.

Photo 15 shows the 3 turned parts.

The clip can now be slipped onto the tenon and the finial is epoxied into the cap tube. It's a good idea to bend the clip mounting ring a little so the clip just touches the body without tension. A quick-grip clamp with soft jaws applies gentle pressure while the glue cures without marring the finish.

Next, the sterling silver ring is glued onto the tenon with epoxy.

Finally, the internal threads need to be glued in place. Apply a small amount of epoxy to the inside of the cap brass tube. Screw the black cap threads tube, seen as a black piece in Photo 16, onto the pen (the grip section and nib may be removed to avoid getting glue on them), with the reduced-diameter end facing the cap. Apply a very small amount of epoxy to it also.

13. The finial needs to be drilled to make room for the nib.

14. Reverse-chuck the finial to shape and finish it.

15. The turned parts for this pen. From left: Main barrel, cap barrel with appropriate tenon for centerband, and cap finial with tenon to fit inside cap barrel tube.

16. Mount the threads on the center coupling and epoxy them into the cap.

I try to make sure I have some glue in the circular grooves, since surface glue will likely be pushed off. Find the best grain alignment and push the two together. Hand pressure should suffice, if the brass tube is clean. Carefully unscrew the pen and wipe off any epoxy that may have been squeezed out.

The pen is done! The techniques I showed should be used as a guide, many variations are possible. The center band does not have to be a sterling silver ring.

You can find suitable center bands all over. You can also turn your own from aluminum, or wood, using any number of decorative techniques. You can turn both barrels closed end, omitting the clip. Of course there are other pen models that lend themselves to these techniques. Models that have a separate, internal, plastic cap thread work best. One example would be the El Grande family, the enlarged ring at the center band fitting can be turned off.

Section IV:
Segmented Pens

19. Basic Segmenting Techniques

In the previous projects the blanks were used as purchased. You can make very interesting pens by creating your own blanks combining materials like wood, veneers, plastic laminates, stone, and other products. You can buy some pre-made segmented pen blanks, but it is fun to make your own. In this chapter, I'll give you some basic elements, and this is by no means exhaustive! There are no limits to what you can create, combining these and other elements in new ways. I will show you some examples in the next two projects. Sometimes you need to build some specialized jigs, but you can also do a lot with the tools and jigs you have. For example, you can rip a pen blank in half on the table saw and sandwich the two halves with veneer(s). If you do that twice at right angles you create the blank shown in Photo 1. Start with a blank that is slightly oversize. This assures that after kerf losses you end up with a usable size. Of course if you use several veneers that add up to the width of the saw blade this is not an issue. Carpenter's glue can be used to laminate woods, or medium or thick CA.

Often it is advantageous to work with long blanks and use a small section at a time. Using a piece of the blank in Photo 1 along with some small veneer pieces, the blank in Photo 2 was created, resulting in the stylish pen shown in Photo 3.

Instead of veneers you might like to use plastic. A popular material is pick-guard, available in sheet form from guitarmaking supply stores. Plastic sheets used for engraving name tags, laminated black-white-black also make a nice effect. I have seen CDs, credit cards, even thin aluminum from soda cans being used. The cuts do not have to be straight. You can make wavy cuts on a scroll saw and sandwich in flexible plastic strips. You can also rip thin strips of wood on the table saw or band saw. The surfaces need to be smooth for gluing. The band saw in particular generally leaves a rough surface that needs to be sanded.

A very simple sanding setup on a drill press is shown in Photo 4. It consists of an inexpensive drum sander (1), a baseboard (2), a fence (3) and a few clamps. The fence should be square to the table. It is clamped front and back. Adjustment is made by loosening the front clamp and making a *small* adjustment. The strips are fed against the rotation. To help feed the

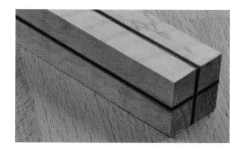

1. Sandwiching some veneers into a blank makes a good starting blank for a segmented pen.

2. Pieces of the blank can be glued up with other elements to create a unique pen blank.

3. A finished segmented pen.

4. With a few blocks of wood you can make a simple thickness sander for creating thin wood strips.

5. Use tape to pull the strips through the sander.

6. The fence is trued to the drum which may not be running like a perfect cylinder.

7. A hexagonal starting blank.

8. The hexagonal glue-up after turning round.

9. Making partial cuts and filling them with wood strips creates an interesting effect.

strips I use some tape to pull them through (Photo 5). It makes sense to make several strips and feed each one through after an adjustment. In reality, such inexpensive drum sanders rarely run true, and because of wobble, you may not get flat strips. One edge may be thicker than the other. You can true the fence to the drum by using a second auxiliary fence and running the real fence past the sander, removing a tiny amount from the surface. Some pencil lines drawn on the surface of the fence will tell you when you have trued the full surface. (Photo 6). This little jig is very useful in producing strips to an exact thickness which are necessary for some designs. The three strips in the picture are of a uniform .050" thickness.

Of course you are not limited to right angles. You can crosscut at an angle and sandwich wood that way, a technique used in the Morning After Pen in Chapter 21. You can also rip some 60° wedges off a board and re-glue them as shown in Photo 7. The wood is clear pine, sandwiched with dyed veneer. After turning the blank round between centers you end up with a starting blank for further customization steps. (Photo 8)

In general, it is better to use close grain, dense woods. When you sand open grain woods the contrasting wood dust can load up some of the grain and give the pen a dirty look. You may have to experiment a little, since some woods also bleed color with certain finishes. Maple, bloodwood, desert ironwood, pink ivory and certain ebonies are amongst my favorites.

10. The filled cuts on a finished pen.

With a softwood, like pine, I try to get a very clean cut with the ½" spindle gouge or the skew, then soak thin CA glue on the blank, saturating the surface. Then you can sand. The CA helps avoid trapping dust from the contrasting wood.

Another element involves making partial cuts on a table saw and filling the kerf with contrasting wood (Photo 9). These cuts are at 60°, and the depth is just less than half the thickness of the blank. If you go over half the thickness, two cuts, on opposite sides, interfere and you can't fully seat the second fill piece. The fill pieces need to be the exact thickness of the kerf. The handy-dandy sanding jig shown in this chapter works well for this. Photo 10 shows the design on a finished pen.

20. Brick Artist's Sketch Pencil

Applying some of the techniques discussed in Chapter 21, we will generate a brick pattern pen. Rip a pen blank in half on the table saw or band saw, and sandwich in a veneer strip using thick CA or carpenter's glue. After it is dry, repeat the process at a right angle, resulting in a blank like Photo 1. Carefully drill the blank along the center where the veneer intersects. Crosscut small sections, about .2" thick, on the band saw or table saw, using a thin kerf blade.

Cut some veneer squares about 1" x 1". If you make them smaller you run the risk of them disintegrating when you drill them. You will need about 17 or 18; make a few extras! To drill them, make a little jig to drill them all at once. Photo 2. It's always a good idea to dry assemble the parts before using glue (Photo 3). For fast cure time, glue on the first section using thick CA and accelerator. Then stack a veneer square followed by the next laminated square, rotating it 45°. Use ample glue. I prefer carpenter's glue here because of longer work time, but thick CA is also usable. With CA you need to apply pressure while you seat each piece. With carpenter glue, you need to make sure you overfill the tube and clamp the whole affair (Photo 4). After the glue dries overnight, square the ends using the pen mill or sanding jig. It is a good idea to soak some thin CA into the last applied piece to make sure it bonds well to the brass tube. In Photo 5 you can see the small gap at the brass tube/

Tools & Materials

- Lathe and standard tooling
- Artist's Sketch Pencil kit (CSU)
- Bushings for Artist's Sketch Pencil
- Pen mill shim barrel (make your own)
- Pen blank ¾ x ¾ x 5", maple
- Veneer or thin wood strips
- $^{15}/_{32}$" drill bit

Note: On the table saw you need to have a zero clearance insert. Even if you have a 10" saw, you can use a thin kerf 7¼" blade which is only ¹/₁₆" thick, to minimize kerf loss. If you use a table saw, it is better to use a blank longer than 5" for safe holding.

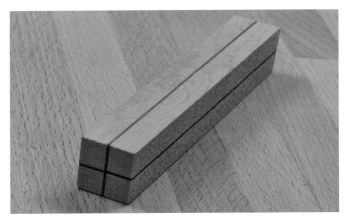

1. Two black veneer strips at right angles sandwiched in a maple blank create the starting blank.

2. A quick jig allows drilling a stack of veneer squares.

3. Dry-assembling the parts is a good idea.

4. Stack the layers, over-filling the blank.

5. The glued-up blank doesn't look like much—yet!

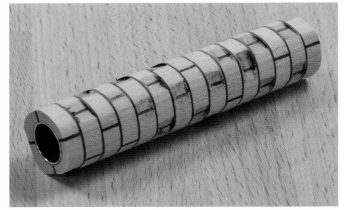

6. If you knock the corners off on a belt sander it is easier to begin turning.

wood bond. Carpenter's glue is not very good at gap filling. If you have a belt or disk sander, knock off the corners to minimize problems during rough turning (Photo 6). After that it's standard fare. Turn to the bushings or the shape of your choice. When turning segmented blanks use light cuts with very sharp tools to avoid unfortunate surprises. I did a CA finish. Assemble the pen according to the kit instructions. The image on page 81 shows the finished pen along with a second pen made from the hexagonal blank shown on page 80.

21. 'Morning After' Pen

The pattern of this project was developed by my friend Ron McIntire who liked to give names to his creations. He called this one "Morning After". This project requires accuracy in sawing, gluing and drilling. The results are stunning and well worth the effort! The pen is made from a precision laminated pen blank made from two contrasting woods, from which you cut wedge shaped sections. The sections are flipped on the pen so contrasting colors oppose each other, and are separated by a third contrasting wood. You end up with a pen that has two very different views, depending upon which side you look at it from. The pen looks very complex, but all the design work is done and Ron was kind enough to share his secrets.

With the sawing jigs I show you here you can make this pen safely. I have used other sawing techniques, like band saw and sander, or a small table saw, but my miter saw does the best job and in the safest way.

Start by creating a ¾ x ¾" blank in contrasting quarters as shown in Photo 1. I use bloodwood and maple here. The quarters have to be exact for the pen to look its best. Because of the many saw cuts, you need a blank for each barrel. Drill one blank dead-center as far as your drill allows with ¹³⁄₃₂" drill the other with the ³¹⁄₆₄". Again, accuracy is essential. The hole needs to be centered, and the drill press table needs to be

Tools & Materials

- Lathe and standard tooling
- Junior Statesman kit (CSU)
- Bushings for Jr. Statesman (CSU)
- Pen mill shim barrels (make your own)
- Two jumbo pen blanks of bloodwood and maple
- Ebony pen blank or similar dark wood
- 12.5 mm (or ³¹⁄₆₄") and 10.5 mm (or ¹³⁄₃₂") drill bits
- Medium or thick CA glue

1. The starting blank for this pen needs to be very exact.

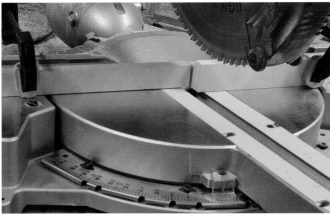

2. The chop saw needs an auxiliary fence and a stop-board.

3. Cutting wedges on the chop saw.

4. Cut thin black wood slices using the same saw setting.

exactly square to the drill axis. To cut the wedges, use the chop saw. Set the saw to the angle you desire; I used about 11.5° here. The exact horizontal angle is not important, but the saw needs to cut exactly vertical. Start with making a zero clearance fence by clamping a board to the saw's fence and taking a cut. Make a stop-board by clamping a second board to the zero clearance fence and cut the edge (Photo 2**)**. Flip the stop-board and set it up to trap the wedge you will cut next. Make a first cut on the blank, then flip the blank, slide it into the stop-board pocket and cut a wedge (Photo 3). To avoid flipping the wedges all over your shop, or damaging them with the blade, make the cut and stop the saw before raising it. Cut sufficient wedges to fill the pen blank.

To make the thin slices between the wedges, drill a blank contrasting wood. Use a 10.5 mm (¹³⁄₃₂") drill to drill from one end of a standard pen blank to the center, then use a 12.5 mm (³¹⁄₆₄") drill to go from the opposite end to the center. This way you can get all the thin slices needed for both barrels. I use Indian ebony here. Flip the stop-board so its edge parallels the saw angle and set it for a narrow width. I added a baseboard to prevent the cut wedge from being flung into the saw blade channel. (Photo 4). Cut the required number of slices. Dry assemble on the brass tube, flipping each wedge so only contrasting colors end up next to each other. After you assemble the first barrel; be sure to orient the first wedge on the second barrel such that the color scheme continues past the center band. If you don't plan that here you may not be able to find an orientation later when you put the pen together, no matter how you flip the barrel. It is best to work from the temporary brass tube onto the final one, transferring one piece at a time while keeping the orientation. Judge how to position the first wedge on the brass tube by centering the tube on the dry assembled stack

5. Dry-assemble on the brass tube and judge how best to center the tube in the blank.

6. The finished barrels, squared and ready for turning.

(Photo 5). Use medium or thick CA to glue up the stack. Even if you use CA let it dry overnight to make sure it is cured not just on the surface—it's very disconcerting seeing a blank disintegrate so close to the end! Square the blanks using the pen mill or sanding jig (Photo 6). If you use a pen mill, it's a good idea to get close by sanding or cutting off on the band saw, to just outside of the brass tube, to avoid the pen mill chewing up the blank.

Knock off the corners on a belt or disk sander (Photo 7). A sharp ½" spindle gouge does a fine job. Take light cuts as with any laminated or segmented blank. Turn to the bushings with the shape of your choice, add a CA or lacquer finish. A friction finish does not work very well on segmented blanks. Assemble according to the instructions. This pen will get you admiring comments wherever you go!

7. Knocking off the corners on the belt sander will make roughing easier.

Section V:
Spirals and Facets

22. Spiraling Jigs

Since the first time I saw ornamental turnings, they have fascinated me. The idea of coupling motions mechanically, by gears and pulleys appeals to me. So when I first saw a jig that could produce spirals on a pen I immediately got the bug and bought one. It was the Beall Master Turner made by the Beall Tool Co. and sold by Woodcraft. Unfortunately, it must be mounted on a mini-lathe. I made only infrequent use of it because I had only one lathe. A few years later I saw another jig sold by Woodcraft, called the MillLathe. It was stand-alone, and I bought one (Photo 1). Instead of gears, it used belts and pulleys. I liked it a lot and made quite a few pens on it. Its Achilles heel is the belt system. You can't push the jig, and it's possible to lose registration because of slipping belts. By that, I mean that if you make 12 parallel spirals on a pen, the 13th should fall exactly into the first, and without a lot of extra care; it does not on the MillLathe. Other than that it is beautifully engineered and still a favorite of mine. This jig has also been discontinued.

Beall came out with another jig, similar to the original Master Turner. It was called the Lathe Wizard and I got one of those since I had a spare mini-lathe at that time. It uses gears and pulleys with timing belts. The belts are cogged so there is no slipping problem. It's a capable system. (Photo 2). For sometime, Legacy Woodturning made a small jig just for pens. It looked like an industrial strength machine but was rather pricey. Their larger machines can also do pens but they take up a lot of floor space and somehow seem to be overkill for the task.

Notice I have talked about a lot of discontinued jigs so far. There is a current jig that you can buy, the Pen Wizard (Photo 3). I mention these older jigs since they do show up at online auctions occasionally, and they all are usable. Most of them had rather skimpy instructions. The Pen Wizard has the best instructions to date, with even a DVD and a decent manual. It also comes fully assembled, unlike its predecessors, and it is stand-alone. Still I think if you are not into tinkering then these jigs are not for you.

1. The MillLathe used belts to synchronize motions. An excellent tool, it is only available on the used tools market now.

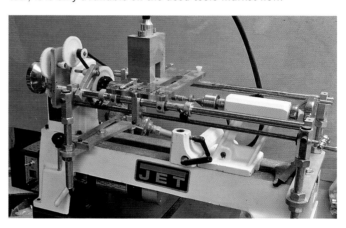

2. The Beall Lathe Wizard. This was a capable tool but is now only available on the used tools market.

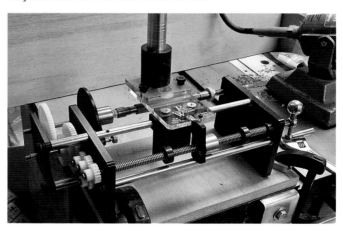

3. The Pen Wizard is a currently manufactured tool for spirals, flutes and wavy patterns.

You have to experiment, figure things out, but you will likely discover things you can do that nobody has done before!

The principle of operation is the same for all of them. You have a hand crank that drives a screw. The screw advances a rotary tool from left to right. At the same time it also drives a reduction system, be that gears or belts. For all but perhaps the Legacy jig this reduction is multi-stage. The last gear in the reduction turns a pen mandrel. So a linear motion is coupled to a rotation, and the relation between them can be set by changing gears or pulleys.

I will use the currently available jig, the Beall Pen Wizard, as an example (Photo 3). The lead screw, that is the screw turned by the crank, has 12 threads per inch. So you have to turn it 12 times to move the cutting tool horizontally by 1". The crank also drives the pen mandrel through a gear reduction. The minimum reduction is 1:3. With this reduction, while you make 12 turns of the crank, the pen mandrel turns ⅓ as many times, i.e. it makes four revolutions, while the cutter has moved 1". This makes a very steep or tight spiral; it has a ¼" pitch. If you set up for a 1:15 reduction, you have to crank 15 times for the pen mandrel to make one full revolution. With the 12 threads-per-inch lead screw, the cutter will have advanced ¹⁵⁄₁₂" or 1¼". The instructions tell you how to set up the gears to achieve various other reductions; you don't really need to figure the gears yourself or get into deep mathematics. The diagram is easy to follow for setup.

I find it hard to classify these tools. They are not toys, but they are also not industrial machines. They have lots of backlash and flex. Yet, if properly set up, they can produce very beautiful pens. Because of the unavoidable backlash, always cut in the same direction, go back to the starting position for each pass after you advance the index. I don't think it's a good idea to retrace a pattern, it often widens the pattern because of inaccuracy.

The next projects use some of these jigs. Typically, any one of them can do similar projects.

Reversing the Pen Wizard

My Pen Wizard, as delivered, was set up so that the workpiece was positioned at the back of the jig. I found that rather awkward. You can turn it around, but then the crank moves from front right to left rear. If you are left-handed, that's great (Photo 4). I am not, so after a hint from JR Beall I decided to reconfigure the jig by building it as a mirror-image. All you need is a ⁷⁄₁₆" wrench and the Allen keys that come with the tool. We start with the machine positioned work front, crank left, rear. First take off the left plate by removing the crank and a couple of nuts. This plate now will become the right plate. Take out the bronze bushing you see in Photo 5 and insert it in the plate from the other side, in the same hole. Take out the center point and also reverse it. Now move the right plate with all the rods attached to the left. Remove one item at a time from the outboard side and remount it inboard (Photo 6). The two shafts in the reverse tumbler also need to be remounted on the other side (Photo 7). Before you re-attach the right side remember to unscrew the tool driver and flip it so the "R" points towards the front (Photo 8). It is not difficult and should be well within the capabilities of anyone that uses this tool. I understand that new Pen Wizards may now be delivered in this configuration.

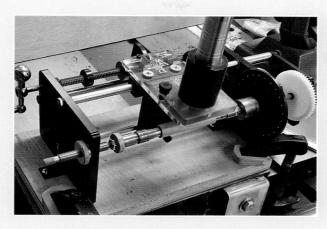

4. The Pen Wizard, turned so the tool is more visible on the operator side.

5. Disassembling the Pen Wizard to convert it to a mirror image for better right-handed operations.

6. Move one item at a time from inside to outside.

7. The reverse tumbler needs to have its shafts flipped.

8. The Acme nut with the tool platform pusher also needs to be reversed so the "R" points forward.

A right-hand and a left-hand spiral.

23. Rope Twist Ballpoint Pen

Rope twist pens always attract attention, I think more so than other spirals. They are actually really easy to make! All you need is a spiraling jig, and a spindle that takes ¼" router bits, such as a Foredom tool. Foredom tools are high quality and carry an appropriate price tag, but there are certainly less expensive alternatives available. I have one that Woodcraft sells. It is largely Foredom compatible and is of decent quality. Many people use spiraling jigs with a Dremel as the cutting tool. These take only ⅛" shaft tools and cannot produce the cut we need for this project. Beall sells a ⅛" rope twist bit, but it is a tiny bit that produces quite a different effect. The cutter we use for this pen is shown in Photo 1. The cutting diameter is ½", and the shape a negative cove. If you make several passes offset by ½" one shape merges with the next and you get flattened half-rounds. Wrap this on a pen as a spiral and you get the illusion of a rope.

To make this work you need to make three passes on a 1.5" pitch or four passes on a 2" pitch. You can also do two passes on a 1" pitch. Try it and see if you like the effect! We are limited by the pitches a given jig can produce. The MillLathe can be set up for a 2" pitch, so four passes will make a nice pen. The Pen Wizard lists pitch a different way. They are listed as "turns per inch." This is just one divided by pitch. There is

Tools & Materials

- Lathe and standard tooling
- Pen Wizard (or other spiral jig)
- ⁷⁄₁₆" wrench
- Foredom tool or similar spindle that takes ¼" router bits
- Rope twist bit, Magnate #7597
- Polaris Pen kit from Penn State Industries
- Polaris bushings
- ¾" pen blank of dense close-grain wood (e.g. bloodwood)
- Mylands cellulose sanding sealer
- Buffing setup

1. A ¼" rope twist bit made by Magnate.

2. The cutter height is set to just above the bushing.

a .64 turns per inch which comes out to 1.54" pitch, close enough to the 1.5" desired. Set up the jig for that, using the instruction book. (The Guilloche attachment needs to be removed first).

The choice of wood is important. I prefer not to do a CA finish on pens with a structured surface like this one. I want to use a wood that cuts well with a router bit and leaves a surface that does not need sanding, or elaborate finishing. Examples of woods that work well are kingwood, African blackwood, bloodwood, desert ironwood, and other woods used in ornamental woodturning. I have some almond wood that also gives excellent results.

The pen is prepared on the lathe. Cut the wood ⅜" longer than the pen tube. Drill down the center with a ⅜" bit and stop before the bit exits. Cut the wood a tad longer than the brass tube, opening the blind hole. Glue in the brass tube with epoxy, and square the ends using a pen mill or sanding jig once the epoxy has cured.

The bushings for the Polaris are .494" and .452". We need to allow for the depth of the cutter profile and would prefer not to cut into the bushing any more than we'll do by accident anyway, so we start by turning a .640" cylinder. Accuracy is not very important, but if you go under .640" you run the risk of having adjacent cuts not join and the rope strands will have flat spots. My jig is not so accurate as to cut

it closer than that. If you have a Morse taper with a ¼-28 thread you could mount the jig's pen mandrel in it, i.e. transfer mandrel, bushings and pen barrel as one unit between machines. I prefer to use my regular pen mandrel and then transfer bushings and barrel to the jig's mandrel.

Mount the larger bushing on the left where the cut starts. Take up the extra space on the mandrel with spare bushings. Screw the brass nut on tight and do snug up the locking hex-nut with a ⁷⁄₁₆" wrench. Vibration tends to loosen nuts! Mount the mandrel in the jig and support its end with the centering point on the right. Do not over tighten it, you'll just distort the side plate. Again use the knurled locknut to make sure it does not vibrate loose. Position and tighten the stop collars such that the cutter clears the pen blank on either side. Adjust the height so the cutter tip is barely above the bushing (Photo 2).

Take the first pass from stop collar to stop collar. You can crank reasonably fast, about two turns of the crank per second. Raise the tool off the work when you return to the left. Advance the index pin eight holes. Make your second pass and repeat one more time after another eight-hole advance. Inspect the results. As long as the pen blank is tight in the mandrel and you know the three index holes you used, you can even take the mandrel off the jig and remount to take another pass with a slightly lowered cutter.

3. The ends are rounded down to the bushings.

4. Buff with the pen angled so the wheel follows the twist direction.

Remove the blank from the mandrel and remount it on the lathe mandrel using the same bushings. Using the spindle gouge or skew, transition the ends to the bushings. If you make a nice clean cut you may not have to sand; otherwise sand the ends you just cut. I don't sand the rope twist area (Photo 3). Turn the speed on low and apply some Mylands cellulose sanding sealer with a cloth, stroking left to right, going at the right speed to pick up the moving spiral. I do about three or four passes. This sealer soaks in the wood and dries very fast. I try to keep the surface wet for 20-30 seconds. When it gets grabby after

the last application I stop. By the time I put the cap on the can, the blank is almost dry. I take it to my buffer and buff with Tripoli, tilting the pen so the buff follows the spiral (Photo 4). Very quickly the blank takes on a great sheen. I repeat this with stage two, white diamond compound. Then follow with a light coat of carnauba wax, also part of the buffing system.

That's it! Assembly of this pen is simple, follow the kit instructions. After the initial setup for the jig, it takes about 15 minutes to make a pen like this. You can also reverse the spiral for left-handed people.

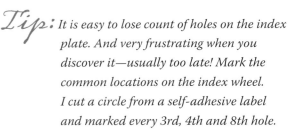

Tip: It is easy to lose count of holes on the index plate. And very frustrating when you discover it—usually too late! Mark the common locations on the index wheel. I cut a circle from a self-adhesive label and marked every 3rd, 4th and 8th hole.

24. Faceted Pen

Faceted pens are actually more difficult than the rope twist pen from the last chapter. The flat faces tend to need more manual sanding or polishing. There is little lathe work involved in making a faceted pen, only the transitions to the bushings. A clever person can design a jig for a router table, something that holds a pen mandrel and is presented to a cutting edge in several fixed orientations. Such jigs have even been available from time to time in various mail-order catalogs. They are usually rather inexpensive. You can also make an adapter for your lathe, a sliding bracket that might hold a trim router. Penn State Industries has such a device available in their catalog. If you have a lathe with index capability (basically a pin that locks the spindle in one of usually 24 positions) these are good options. All the spiraling jigs can be used in this mode; here I will use the MillLathe.

Start as usual, glue a brass tube into the blank and square the faces. In theory you could use the full blank and let the router cutter do all the work, but in reality this puts a lot of stress on the jig and will lead to lots of vibration. So you could do it in stages, a rough pass followed by a final pass. However, turning the blank round to a diameter just a little larger than you need is much more efficient. Mathematically inclined pen makers can use some basic trigonometry to figure out the needed diameter. For the octagonal pen that we will make just add 15% or a little more to the bushing diameter and this will be close enough. The Sierra bushings are .474", so roughly .550" is a good diameter. The second consideration is what bit to use. The bit has to be larger than the flats we make; ¼" is plenty for the Sierra pen. A larger diameter bit will also work

Tools & Materials

- Lathe and standard tooling
- Spiral jig
- Foredom tool or similar tool using ¼" bits
- ¼" end mill
- Sierra Pen kit from Berea
- Sierra bushings
- ¾" pen blank of dense close-grain wood
- Mylands cellulose sanding sealer
- Buffing setup with Tripoli, white diamond (and optionally carnauba wax)

1. The belts, or gears, are removed and the mandrel held fixed while the cutter travels across, cutting with the end face. All jigs are capable of this cut.

2. Sand one face at a time on a flat surface.

3. Turn a transition down to the bushing.

4. Double-barrelled pens are just twice as much sanding work. Adding a little slope enhances the appearance.

but it will produce more vibration. Any router bit that cuts a flat bottom will work. I like the end-mill style with solid carbide cutters.

Mount the blank(s) on the jig. I have room for two so I set up two here. Disengage the gears. On the MillLathe that means the belts are removed. Set up the end stops on the lead screw. Lock the spindle via any one of the index holes. Position the cutter a little bit away from the bushing. Take a cut across the blanks, return with the cutter retracted to the origin and rotate the blank by three index holes. If your cutter travels from right to left, by rotating the blank *towards* you, the cutter will cut into the previous flat on the next pass and the fuzzy tearout it leaves will always be removed by the next cut. Thus, less cleanup work! Remove the blank from the jig. To sand the sides, slide the blank across sand paper on a flat surface. A good starting grit would be 320. Put a finger on top of the blank. After some back and forth strokes, rotate the blank over the edge onto the next facet and give the same number of strokes (Photo 2). Do this for all eight facets. After you have removed all the tool marks with 320 grit, apply Mylands cellulose

sanding sealer with a paper towel, rag, or brush. Keep the blank wet for about half a minute to a minute, reapplying sealer. The sealer dries within a few minutes. Now proceed to the next sand paper grade. I go through 400, 600, 800 and 1200 grit.

Put the blank back on the lathe and make a transition to the bushings using your favorite tool, a spindle gouge or skew works well (Photo 3). Now, take the blank to the buffer and go through Tripoli and white diamond, followed by carnauba wax if you want. Try to preserve the hard edges by polishing mainly lengthwise especially with the Tripoli. Assemble the pen according to the instructions. The Sierra is very simple to put together.

Note that with some jigs you can put a taper on the barrel also. The Pen Wizard can do it but you have to make a pattern for the carriage to follow, and because the cutter itself does not tilt the flat will become a slight cove which you have to remove by sanding. The Lathe Wizard and the MillLathe can produce perfect flats on a taper. The Junior Gentleman's pen in Photo 4 is an example.

25. Fluted Pen

Flutes are very easy to do on a spiraling jig! I used the Beall Pen Wizard here. All other spiral jigs can also do flutes, some even a little more easily. The Pen Wizard is a little cramped to work on (a trade-off for compact size), and has a fair amount of flex and backlash, which means a little extra care needs to be taken to compensate. For flutes you need a small bit, so a Dremel tool works very well. I'm usually set up with the Foredom. It can take small bits with an appropriate collet. You can make flutes using a bit with a round end, and just polish them, or you can fill the grooves with a suitable contrasting material. For filling grooves a square end is better.

I chose the Electra kit here because it has a long body that looks good with flutes. Also I don't have to worry about pattern alignment between body and cap since the Electra has a metal cap. Start by preparing the blank in the usual way: Cut the blank ⅜" longer than the brass tube, drill without breaking through the end, then cut a tad longer than the brass tube exposing the end of the drilled hole. Glue in the brass tube with epoxy and square the ends using a pen mill with appropriate sleeve or a sanding jig. Turn the blank to the bushings. If the wood has open grain or areas where filling material (crushed stone) might accidentally get into, apply a sanding sealer or a coat of thin CA. You don't even have to sand. The final turning occurs later after the grooves are cut and filled.

Set up the spiraling jig for flutes. On the Pen Wizard, remove one of the small gears (1 in Photo 1) so that the gear train will not try to turn the spindle. The Guilloche attachment may stay in place. The actual locking though is done via the large sliding gear (2 in Photo 1) that is moved out

Tools & Materials

- Lathe and standard tooling
- Spiral jig
- Foredom or Dremel tool using ⅛" bits
- ⅛" end mill
- Electra Pen kit from Berea
- Electra bushings
- ¾" pen blank of dense close-grain wood (amboyna burl)
- 10.5 mm or "Z" drill bit
- Crushed turquoise stone
- CA thin and medium

1. On the Pen Wizard the spindle gear (1) is removed to decouple the motion, and the sliding gear (2) is moved to the right to lock the spindle.

2. It is a good idea to use a spare tube to set the depth of the flute cut.

3. For the plunge cuts, push the cutter to the same side for every cut.

for Guilloche pattern cutting. Make sure this gear is moved in and engages the spindle. Keeping the Guilloche attachment in place provides a better lock even with a gear setup that offers little resistance.

Before mounting the pen body on the Pen Wizard it is a good idea to use a spare Electra brass tube to set the cutting depth. Mount the tube on the jig using the Electra bushings (Photo 2). Set the rotary tool so it is centered over the brass tube and use the thumb screw to set the height so that the cutter just misses the tube. If you forget that step, it is somewhat difficult to judge later how deep the cut should be. If you cut through the brass tube, you may end up with an interesting pen but you will not be able to fill the groove with stone!

Remove the brass tube and substitute the pen barrel. Set the end stops to keep the cutter away from the

barrel ends. We will cut six grooves so every fourth hole will be used. Cut the first groove, lift out the cutter and return to the start. Advance the index four holes and cut the next groove until done. Marking the index wheel for every fourth dot is very helpful.

To add an offset decorative dot, reset the end stops to let you move closer to the end, and plunge the holes using the in between index holes. The Pen Wizard has a lot of slop; mine has more than $\frac{1}{16}$". Such variation could destroy a pattern, so be sure to hold the tool to the same side of the slop for every plunge cut (Photo 3).

Remove the barrel from the jig and mount it on the lathe mandrel with the bushings. Fill the grooves with crushed stone (Photo 4). Try to fill the grooves to the top, manipulate the stone using a dental pick or toothpick to get it level. If you overfill you just have to turn it down again, and stone is hard. There should not be any gaps where you can see the bottom of the groove. Now add thin CA glue to lock the stone in place. Use a micro-tip on the glue bottle. Don't let it touch the stone itself, just hold it to the edge and let the CA come out very slowly and wick into the stone (Photo 5). If you add CA too fast the stone can float away. You want just enough thin CA to hold the stone in place. Work around all the grooves and accents.

Add medium CA to over fill the features now. Once it is cured turn back down to the wood. The stone filled grooves should be completely covered with CA now. If you over filled the grooves with stone, your HSS tool may get dull very quickly, so a carbide tipped

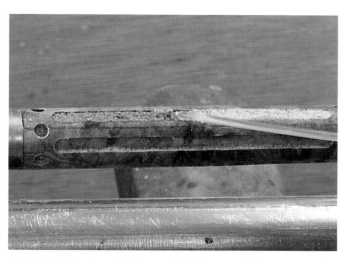

4. The grooves are filled level with crushed turquoise.

5. Let thin CA glue wick in carefully. The nozzle does not touch the stone.

tool might be best. But HSS works with a little honing along the way.

Add a CA finish. My best finish these days (and yes, it is still changing!) is the wet polished medium CA. Apply CA as shown in Chapter 6, sand and scrape it as shown. Instead of continuing into dry polishing, I wet polish the CA as shown on acrylic in Chapter 12, all the way through micro-mesh 12,000. Assemble the

pen according to the instructions, making sure the nib is aligned with the nicest stone groove, and start showing it off proudly.

Of course, the same stone fill technique can be used on spiral grooves. There are alternatives to crushed stone also. Glitter and brass powder are some media my friends have used. I like the textured look crushed stone offers.

Tip: Turn a wood handle and mount a 7 mm brass tube in it.
Cut away part of the brass tube on a sander and you have
a great small scoop for applying crushed stone with minimal waste.

26. Spiral-Grooved Pen

Spirals are what a spiraling jig is all about, of course. There are many effects you can achieve depending on the bit used and some of the pattern determining parameters such as the gearing and number of repetitions around the pen, as well as mixing left and right spirals. I have had most success with low profile spirals, and in particular slow spirals that look less like a screw thread and more like a slow twist. For this project, I used the Pen Wizard, the jig currently available on the market. The Pen Wizard allows a slow spiral. The manual shows the gearing for .12 turns per inch. In reality, this pitch is .16 but it really does not matter. It is a slow twist, about a full revolution in 6". Set up the gearing using the greatest reduction you can get on the jig. From the drive shaft, always use the smallest gear to interlock with the largest. Photo 1 shows the gearbox with the plate removed.

I will use an acrylic pen blank for this project. Acrylics are challenging to work with. It is best to try your spiral cuts on scrap before committing to the actual work. One way to do this is to turn the barrel round and make your test cuts on it, optimizing cutter RPM and feed rate. Then take the blank off again, turn it to shape and make the real cuts. You typically need a slower RPM for plastics than for wood. Fast feed rates help. You need to avoid melting the plastic. Some resins with low melting points are not suitable for this type of work—luckily, there are

Tools & Materials

- Lathe and standard tooling
- Spiral jig
- Foredom or Dremel tool using ⅛" bits
- ⅛" engraving bit
- Polaris Click pen kit from Penn State Industries
- Polaris Click bushings
- ⅜" drill bit
- ¾" acrylic acetate pen blank

1. A gearing setup for a slow twist. Always arranged from the smallest cog to the largest.

2. An engraving bit has a very sharp point.

3. The bit is set to protrude a tiny amount below the depth guide.

plenty that are. The blank I used here came from Craft Supplies USA.

Prepare the blank the usual way. Cut the blank ⅜" longer than the brass tube. Drill without breaking through the end, and then cut a tad longer than the brass tube exposing the end of the drilled hole. Paint the inside of the blank with a matching paint to avoid having the brass tube show through on the pen (see Chapter 8). Glue in the brass tube with epoxy and square the ends using a pen mill with the appropriate sleeve, or a sanding jig. Turn to a shape you like. The Pen Wizard has an accessory that rides on the pen blank and follows the shape. Sand to remove tool marks. Final sanding and polishing will happen later, but you want a smooth surface for the depth guide to ride on. Move the pen blank and bushings over onto the spiral jig and lock it securely on the mandrel. Set up the stops so the bit does not run into

the bushings. Mount the engraving bit in the rotary tool. Photo 2 shows a patterning bit. The point is very sharp! Center the tool over the work and within the slot of the depth guide. The tool should protrude a very tiny amount, approximately ¼₄" below the depth guide (Photo 3). Move the tool to the start position, lower it into the work and make your first groove with the setting you found. Remember that plastic materials are different. Some are just not usable for this decoration since they melt around the bit.

At the end of the cut raise the tool and move it back to the starting position. Advance the index by two holes and make the next cut. Continue to make a total of 12 cuts. The blank will not look pretty at this point—don't worry, it'll get there!

As you move the pen barrel back to the lathe you can knock most of the surface fuzz off with your fingers. A quick pass with 600 grit sand paper will restore the surface and hard edges along the grooves. It is best to scrape out the grooves with a couple of toothpicks or a dental pick because the shavings trapped there will come out during wet polishing. Wet polish with micro-mesh from 1500 to 12000. Use longitudinal strokes before you advance to the next grit. Also lengthwise drying with a soft cotton cloth after each step will keep the grooves clean. You can fill the grooves but I like the understated contrast of the unpolished grooves to the highly polished surface so I leave it as is. For filling, you can use water based acrylic artist's paint. Apply it with a cloth, packing it in the grooves while wiping the surface clean with a damp rag. Another suitable product for filling is "Rub'n Buff," a wax available in craft supply stores.

4. After grooving, the blank looks very rough.

Assembly of this pen is not difficult but you have to follow the instructions carefully. Construction is a little unusual since a threaded bushing has to be inserted exactly 18.5 mm from the upper end into the brass tube. The kit contains a short disposable piece of tubing of the proper length. The decorative rings need to be assembled in just the right order with the clip. Note that the two rhodium-plated rings are not the same. One of them has a recess for the clip.

Occasionally I have had some issues with the mechanism not working 100% of the time. Every once in a while the refill would not retract. I thought it was an error in the way I put the pen together. Finally I figured out the cause of the problem and a simple fix which I now apply as preventive measure on every Click Polaris. The travel of the button is restricted if assembled as designed. To assure reliable operation, remove the pusher button but leave the click mechanism and spring in the pen (Photo 5). Add a bit of epoxy to the female thread inside the button.

5. Remove the button for a preemptive correction to a sticking mechanism.

Then screw it back onto the pen, but back it out half a turn from where it stops and let the epoxy dry there. Since using this simple fix I have had no problems with this pen.

A beautiful pen that you can show off proudly!

Tip: *The disposable tube that comes with the kit gets the job done but starting it is a little awkward. It seems like you need three hands to keep the parts aligned. You can make a custom tool on the wood lathe, out of ½" aluminum rod, for pushing the threaded bushing 18.5 mm (= 0.728") down into the brass tube (Photo 5). I turned the aluminum with a spindle gouge and made the shoulders with a parting tool.*

A simple tool to position the internal click mechanism mount, can be turned from ½" aluminum.

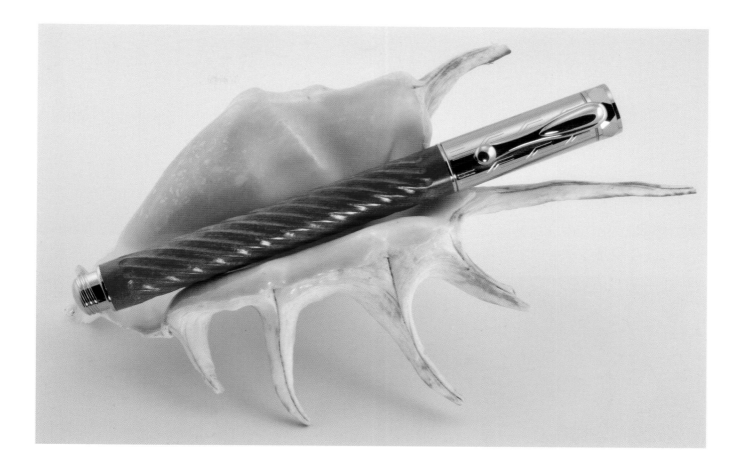

27. Cove-Spiral Pen

When designing a spiral pen, there are lots of options. To come up with something that looks good really means experimentation. You can vary the pitch of the spiral by changing the gearing. You can also achieve very different looks by the cutter bit you use. In Chapter 26 we used an engraving bit to make narrow lines. Chapter 23 showed a rope twist effect; the cutter bit dictated a specific pitch for this to work out. Also the depth of the cut is pre-determined. In this project we will use a ball-end mill to make cove cuts where the grooves join in a cusp. There are lots of parameters at our disposal! Of course we are limited by the thickness of the wood since we don't want to cut into the brass tube.

Note: The Stretch is available from Lau Lau Woodworks. It is also available as Gran Torino from Arizona Silhouette, and now as Electra from Berea Hardwoods and their distributors. It is the same pen, but offered in different platings from the various sources.

Tools & Materials

- Lathe and standard tooling
- Spiral jig
- Foredom or Dremel with ¼" ball-end bit
- Stretch pen kit
- Stretch bushings (or Electra Bushings)
- 10.5 mm or "Z" drill bit
- ¾" pen blank (dense closed grain hardwood)

1. Ball-end cutters from ½" to ⅛" diameters.

2. Test cuts are necessary to find the right settings.

22
60
50
12

3. Gearing for .35 turns/inch (roughly 3" pitch).

4. Make all passes from left to right to avoid backlash.

Ball-end cutters come in a variety of diameters (Photo 1). To develop a new pattern you have to sacrifice some wood (Photo 2). Rather than glue up a blank every time we will use a loose brass tube so it can be re-used. The best drill bit for the Gran Torino is 10.5 mm or "Z", but since we don't need to allow for glue, a test blank is drilled with ¹³⁄₃₂" which is a tight fit. Slide in the brass tube without glue, mount it on the bushings and turn it round. Then move it to the spiral jig.

> *Tip:* *When you set up the gearing on the Pen Wizard make sure the gears don't touch. The gears slide on the axles, and if their faces touch you can get a jerky motion. You may also feel higher resistance on the crank.*

Remove the depth follower and Guilloche attachment from the jig. Center the cutter over the blank and set the end stops, preventing the cutter from running into the bushings.

Find a pitch and depth that you like. You don't have to turn a complete pen every setting, usually by the third pass you can see the effects. If you go to the tighter pitch (in Pen Wizard terminology, more turns per inch) the coves move closer together or get narrower. If you increase the depth, the height of the cusps between adjacent grooves decreases. I wanted to have the cusps rather close to the original pen surface so it took several iterations to get it right. I ended up with a .35 turns/inch (or a pitch of around 3"), and 12 passes, i.e. using every other hole on the index plate, using a ¼" ball-end mill. Photo 3 shows the gearing.

Note: If you use larger diameter cutters, like a ½" with a ¼" shank to fit the Foredom, the cutter will tend to want to skip along the surface rather than cut a shallow cove in a gravity system like the Pen Wizard's or the Lathe Wizard. On the MillLathe or the Master Turner the cutter is mechanically driven into the wood and this is not an issue.

Prepare your blank. Choose a dense, close grain wood that cuts cleanly. I used pink ivory here. After the time involved in dialing in a cut like this it makes sense to make more than one pen! Cut the blank ⅜" longer than the brass tube, drill using a 10.5 mm or "Z" bit, without breaking through

5. Angle the pen on the buffer so as to buff along the grooves and keep the ridges crisp.

the end, then cut a bit longer than the brass tube exposing the end of the drilled hole. Glue in the brass tube with epoxy and square the ends using a pen mill with the appropriate sleeve, or a sanding jig. Turn the pen to the bushings. Sand and polish near the bushings, the rest of the pen will get a new surface.

Move to the spiral jig and lock the blank and bushings securely. Take your cuts, cutting only on the left-to-right pass (Photo 4). Move back to the lathe. Apply Mylands cellulose sanding sealer with a brush or

piece of cloth, keep the surface wet for half a minute to a minute, then wipe off all of the excess with a rag. Let the pen sit for a few minutes, then move to the buffing wheel and buff through Tripoli, white diamond and carnauba wax (Photo 5), angling the pen so the wheel polishes in the direction of the coves. Assemble the pen following the instructions, sit back and relax, admiring your beautiful pen. Then go make a few more!

Section VI:
The Metal Lathe in the Pen Shop

28. Equipment

Metal lathes open a whole new world to the pen maker. It is not so much the ability to turn metal (though this does come in very handy) as the ability to make threads and work to tolerances not easily held on wood lathes. A lot has happened since I first worked on a metal lathe in high school shop. These days you can buy a Chinese-made metal lathe for around $300 and it is anything but a toy. Of course, your work envelope is limited, but we are making pens! Also, for $300 you don't get the same quality as a precision model shop lathe, but if you put in the effort to tune and improve it, it can do very good work. I had an inexpensive Chinese 7x12 lathe as a first lathe for quite a few years and learned a lot on it.

1. An inexpensive, yet very capable Chinese lathe.

When thinking about a metal lathe, and as you search the web for advice, several options usually come up. There are small lathes like Sherline and Taig. They are great model making lathes, and may serve your need. But you are buying into a closed system. Sherline accessories are expensive. I opted for the 7x12 because it had more capacity all around. It also used more standard parts that were available from more than one source. In addition, it is heavier, which I considered an asset in a lathe. The smaller Chinese lathe commonly available is the 7x10, and I would advise considering a 7x12 for approximately the same money which is nearly identical to the 7x10 but has a 4" longer bed. No kidding! Some suppliers do call it a 7x14 also. For a little bit more money I would highly suggest the 8x12 available from Harbor Freight (Photo 1) which was my second lathe. It is substantially heavier, can do larger work and take bigger cuts, and

is generally a much better built lathe. It goes on sale for under $500 quite frequently. The field is constantly changing, of course, new models with better specs and more capacity will keep appearing.

From there, it goes up; larger lathes, higher precision and higher price. One thing you need to keep in mind is that there is an endless array of accessories you will "need" as time goes on. And while some tools are really essential, others make life easier. I have not had the need to use a steady or traveling rest. Usually my work is close to the headstock or supported by a center. A live center is a must-have, as is a drill chuck for your tailstock. A four-independent-jaw chuck is capable of higher precision than most three-jaw chucks have. A pair of calipers is essential, as is a dial test indicator with magnetic stand. You need cutting tools and a grinder. I have not had good luck with brazed carbide tools. The cheap ones seem to chip very easily which renders them useless. Some high-speed steel (HSS) tools are good to have; however, my preference is carbide insert tools. A quick-change tool

2. Lathe tooling: (1) dial test indicator with magnetic stand, (2) machinist's protractor, (3) fishtail gauge, (4) indexable tools, (5) calipers, (6) 0-1" micrometer, (7) collet chuck with ER32 collets, (8) tap center, (9) tap holder, (10) deburring tool, (11) HSS tools, (12) boring bar, (13) drill chuck for tailstock, (14) tailstock die holder, (15) revolving center, (16) cutting fluid.

post is a wonderful accessory that I would not want to be without. A reasonable quality 1" micrometer is a good investment. It does not have to be electronic. I have a mechanical digital micrometer that did not cost much and it has served me well. Photo 2 shows some of the essential tools. I would highly recommend a collet chuck. I use ER32 collets on my wood lathe, and the same collets can be held on the metal lathe with a collet chuck that mounts in the spindle (typically Morse-taper 3 on this class lathe). Not only does it give repeatable accuracy, but also each collet has a holding range of .040", unlike many other collet systems where each collet can only hold a fixed diameter accurately. It also lets you hold tubing material without crushing. You will certainly need HSS center drills; the ones with a 60-degree countersink are the most useful.

You can turn wood on a metal lathe though I generally don't. I think sawdust and oil and metal shavings are not a great combination. Most metal lathes also don't spin as fast as wood lathes so finishing techniques would need to be adapted. Since I do have a wood lathe I split the jobs as needed. You can buy or make an accessory tool rest for a metal lathe that lets you use your wood chisels and if this is your only lathe it is a great compromise.

I am not a machinist. I am mostly self-taught though I have machinist friends at my day job that have given me excellent advice. So I am hardly in a position to teach the ins and outs of using a metal lathe. There is a lot of information available on the Internet, and all of these smaller lathes have user groups with lots of help. I will show you some practical applications the way I do them. I will mostly use the 8x12 lathe though I do have a larger Emco Mayer lathe that gets more use. The 8x12 is capable of doing everything although sometimes with a little more effort compared to my big lathe. Sometimes it does it better. For example, I installed a crank to the spindle of the 8x12 that I do not have on the large lathe, and for threading, it is much easier to use.

29. Mandrels

Mandrels are very easy to make and a good first project. An "A" mandrel can be made from size "D" drill rod. Drill rod is available in 3' lengths and is inexpensive. The main cost is usually shipping so if you can pick it up locally, so much the better. It is available as air-hardening, oil-hardening or water-hardening. Get the cheapest! The steel compositions are slightly different, and the oil/air/water refers to the type of cooling after heat treatment. I have never hardened a mandrel. Dimensionally they are equivalent, as well as in terms of stiffness.

Cut an 8" section with a hacksaw. Mount it in the lathe chuck, leaving about ½" showing in front of the jaws, and measure the runout with a dial test indicator. The three-jaw chuck has three pinions that can be tightened. They may not give the same degree of concentric accuracy! Experiment to determine if you can achieve non-measurable runout. You really want less than .001" (Photo 1). If you can't get that, use the four-jaw chuck. A four-jaw chuck allows you to dial out any runout. Basically you adjust a pair of opposing jaws at a time, loosen one jaw and tighten the opposite one till you achieve the accuracy you need. You can dial out any runout that way. Some collet holders have a through-hole so you can mount the rod with only

> *Tip:* *Runout is a term used to measure concentricity. The correct technical term is Total Indicated Runout or TIR. It gets a bit confusing because TIR is also used as an abbreviation for Total Indicator Readout. Not wanting to get lost in metrology details, I use the term runout somewhat loosely here. Mount a polished rod in the lathe chuck. A commercial "drill blank" makes a good polished rod. Set the indicator close to the chuck jaws to avoid other errors that creep in as you move further out. Turn the chuck through a full rotation by hand and make a note of the high and low readings. The difference is what I call runout here.*

a small piece showing, that's usually the best option. Make sure your cutting tool is the proper height, right on center, and turn the end face flat.

Use a #2 combined center drill/60-degree countersink in the tailstock mounted drill chuck to drill a hole in the drill rod. Put a drop of cutting oil on the drill to avoid breaking it. Drill until you start developing

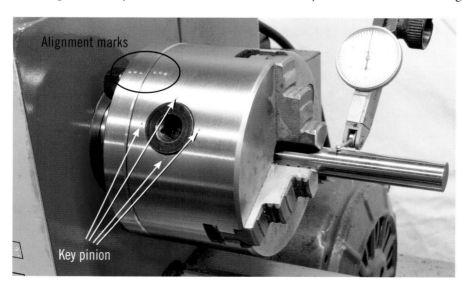

1. Mark the mounting position of the three jaw chuck and the key pinion that give the lowest runout.

2. A center drill, combined with a 60 degree countersink, creates the surface for the live center to run on. On the outside, add a chamfer using a file to let the die start easier.

3. A die holder is essential to cut male threads.

a shoulder with the 60-degree flanks of the bit. This 60-degree shoulder is where the center will fit. Take a file and carefully file a chamfer on the exposed end (Photo 2).

Move the drill rod out until you have about 2" showing. You do not need the same degree of accuracy now. Mount the ¼ x 28 TPI die in the die holder and the die holder guide in the tailstock. Note that the die has printing on one side only, this is the side you want showing, facing the work. Put some cutting oil on the drill rod and on the teeth of the die. You can cut under power (Photo 3), with the lathe on slow, holding the die holder by hand, or by turning the chuck by hand using the chuck wrench as a handle. Cut about 1". Try to slide on a bushing. Usually you will find a burr where the thread stops. You must remove that with a small file. Work with the file until the bushings or a 7 mm brass tube slide on easily. Add the nut and the business end is done! The reason we chose the ¼-28 fine thread instead of the ¼-20 is that the threads are not as deep and thus easier to cut.

Turn the mandrel around, face off the other end, use a file to remove the burr and add a small chamfer at the end. This completes the mandrel!

A "B" mandrel can be made from size L (0.290") drill rod. The process is nearly identical. You again start by making the small center dimple with the center drill. Then you need to turn about a 1" length to a ¼" diameter. You should support the drill rod using a live center in the dimple you just made. Then you can cut the ¼ x 28 thread and face off the other end and you're done!

If you are making mandrels, you don't have to stay with the standard sizes. For example, if you will be making large pens, why not use a ⅜" mandrel? If you don't want to make your own bushings, you can still use commercial ones, you just need to open them up to fit. The next chapter will deal with bushings. A ⅜" mandrel is 132% stiffer than an "A" mandrel and 67% stiffer than a "B" mandrel.

Tip: The tool height is right when there is no nipple left in the center of an end face cut. Use shims to get the tool to the proper height. Another good way to set the height is by using a thin 6" ruler. Advance the tool against some round stock and put a 6" ruler between tool and stock. If the ruler is vertical, the height is correct.

30. Bushings

A bushing is an accessory that is simple to make. The first set may take you an evening, but once you get comfortable, you can probably do a set in less than a half-hour. With the cost of commercial bushings, you may ask why do it at all. I have to admit that in my shop sometimes things get lost. So I have the option of searching for an hour or more with no guarantee of success, ordering a set and waiting a few days, or make a quick set. Besides, metalworking is fun! The steps are quite simple.

First, you need to measure the hardware fittings to find the large diameter of the bushings. We'll use the El Grande as an example here, making a cap bushing. Do not trust the diameter you may find printed in some of the instruction sheets! I have seen incorrect diameters printed on instructions more than once. You also need to measure the inside diameter of the brass tube for the smaller bushing diameter. My measurements are .590" and .494".

Cut a piece of ⅝" or ¾" steel about 4" in length. Mount it in the three-jaw chuck, leaving about 1" protruding in front of the jaws. It does not matter if it runs true; all operations will be done without remounting.

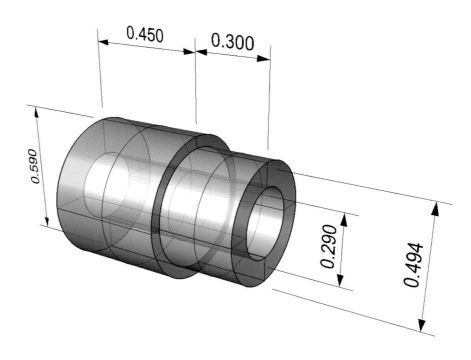

Square the front surface by taking successive small cuts using the cross slide. Do this until the surface is clean; i.e. there are no unmachined areas. This operation is called facing. Use the center drill (with a drop of cutting oil) in the tailstock chuck and drill a dimple into the end. The center drill is accurately ground and will pull into the true center. Switch to a "K" drill bit and drill about .7" deep. Lathe speed for these operations might be around 400–600. Now mount the "L" chucking reamer in the tailstock and

Other Materials for Bushings

You can also make bushings out of plastic materials. They may not last as long so you may want to use them just for finishing. I like Delrin as a material. It is readily available, cuts easily and is quite stable. And CA does not readily adhere to it. Some other plastics like polypropylene are even more resistant to glue but they are soft and difficult to machine accurately.

Tools & Materials

- Metal lathe with standard accessories
- ⅝" steel rod, 4" long
- Center drill
- Drill bit size "K"
- Chucking reamer size "L"

ream the hole to the exact diameter, using cutting oil again. Withdraw the reamer with the lathe still running. Never pull out a reamer while the lathe is stopped or even worse, turning backwards.

Turn the outside diameter to 0.590" for a length of ¾". If the compound is set parallel to the ways there is less chance of accidentally changing the diameter. Either set the cross slide dial to 0 on the final pass or write down the setting. Turn the step to a diameter of .494" for a length of about 0.3". I use the scale on the cross slide to turn to .500" (removing .090" diameter from the last setting, in several passes) and check with a micrometer. It should read .500". Remove .006" with the final pass. Use a file to put a little chamfer on the end, with the lathe running. Check to see if the brass tube slips on. Now use a parting tool right next to the step at .75" and part off the bushing. Before removing the remaining bar, face off the end, removing any evidence of the previously drilled hole. If you do not do that and just try to extend the hole for the next bushing the hole will almost certainly be off-axis. Reverse-mount the bushing on the large diameter and deburr the exit hole. Clean the bushing

Steel Types

There are many different steels and they differ widely in their workability. The easiest steel to work with that I know of is called 12L14. It is steel containing some lead and cuts extremely well. Drill rod as used for the mandrel is workable but harder to get a good surface on. However, it is readily available in many diameters. Stainless steel of type 303 is one of the easier stainless steel alloys to work with. It cuts very well, especially with carbide tools, even on a small metal lathe.

and try it on the mandrel. At times, you may have to do a bit more deburring.

Remount the rod and repeat for the next bushing! If you want to make bushings for an "A" mandrel use a "C" drill bit and a "D" reamer. When making Delrin bushings, I get better results with a reamer that is a little oversize: .291" for a "B" mandrel or .247" for an "A" mandrel.

31. Expansion Mandrel

An expansion mandrel is not difficult to make. It is a cone section drawn by a bolt into a slotted tube that expands as the cone is drawn in. It is very similar to the way a bicycle's handlebar stem used to be. Photo 1 shows a disassembled expansion mandrel. The anatomy is quite obvious. Quite a few expansion mandrels (a.k.a. closed end mandrels) are available commercially now from Arizona Silhouette. However, there are always new kits coming around that don't fit available mandrels. Here I am making a mandrel for an Ambassador cap, which, incidentally, also fits the Gentleman/Statesman pen. The ID of the brass tube is .550".

Commercial expansion mandrels tend to have a sizing bushing. I never make one, but use calipers instead. A sizing bushing requires extra space on the mandrel, and can be a nuisance if you use a CA finish.

Start by making the draw bar. Chuck up a piece of ¼" steel drill rod, 4½" long. Use a ¼-28 die in a die holder mounted in the tailstock to cut a thread about ½" long on one end, and 1" long on the other. You can

also use a length of ¼-28 all thread. ¼-20 all thread may be easier to find and is OK to use. The challenge with the coarser thread is tapping the hole without having the work slip in the chuck.

I make the main body out of type 303 stainless steel alloy, chosen for its easy machinability. I also use 12L14 but it rusts, so 303 is my preference if I have it on hand. Drill rod is another alternative although I find it harder to get a good finish on it. From a functionality perspective, it is fine; in the end, it's just a tool! Chuck up a 4½" (approximately) section of ⅝" rod, leaving at least 2¼" protruding past the jaws/collet. Make sure it has no, or very little, runout! A four-jaw chuck easily lets you get less than .001" runout. Face the end and center drill it. Drill with a #3 drill to a depth of about ½". Using thread cutting oil, and without lathe power, tap the hole with a ¼-28 tap, using a tap center to keep it straight (Photo 2). Turn a ¼" section to a diameter a little less than the tube ID, about .540". Swing the compound to about 80 degrees, which makes it 10 degrees off parallel to

1. Anatomy of an expansion mandrel. (1) tapered expansion plug, (2) draw bar, (3) nut, (4) main body with slotted end.

Tools & Materials

- Metal lathe with standard accessories
- ⅝" steel rod, about 4½" long
- ¼" drill rod 4½" long
- ¼" airline drill (6" or 8" long)
- Centering drill
- ¼" NF die
- Die holder for lathe tailstock
- ¼" NF tap
- Tap center
- #3 drill
- Cutting oil
- Loctite red
- Hacksaw, file

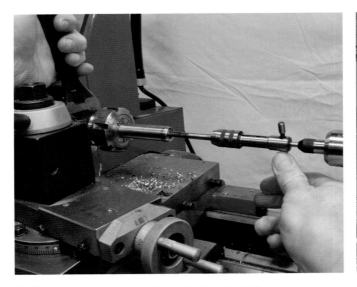

2. Use a tapping center to keep the tap straight.

3. Run the lathe in reverse and work on the back of the workpiece to cut the taper with the compound.

4. A boring bar cuts the internal taper with the same compound setting.

the ways. Running the lathe in reverse, and with the tool behind the work, cut a taper on the tenon you just turned, using the compound (Photo 3). Use a parting tool to remove the taper. This will be the plug (item 1 in Photo 1. Attach it to the draw bar after putting a drop of red Loctite on the threads. Once the Loctite is dry, it holds the taper on securely.

Drill all the way through the body with the ¼" airline drill. The lathe speed should be somewhat slow like 300-500 RPM. Use cutting oil. I was amazed that the long drill remains accurately centered as long as the lathe is slow, you advance the bit slowly, and use plenty of cutting oil. Once the chips stop ejecting you'll have to withdraw the drill bit every ¼" or so.

Reduce the diameter to .550" for a length of 2.2". The brass tube length is 2.05", this leaves a .15" gap to the mandrel step which I find sufficient. Take small cuts since the tube is unsupported at the end. Test that the brass tube slips on but fits snugly. You can reduce the diameter a little more in the middle if you like, such that the tube is only supported at the ends. This may help getting a good slide fit. Polish the seating surfaces with sandpaper.

Open the draw bar hole to ⁷⁄₁₆" and a depth of about ¾". It is best to work up through a couple of drill sizes. Use a boring bar and the compound feed (which is still at the same angle we turned the taper

plug with) and make a mating internal taper, this time working on the front with the lathe running forward, of course (Photo 4). Now cut a slot to the depth of the ⁷⁄₁₆" hole using a hack saw or band saw. I find a 4 x 6 band saw an excellent addition to a metal workshop (Photo 5). Remove any burr using a file and re-test the brass tube slip fit. File or grind two flats on the end for a wrench. Add a ¼-28 nut and washer to the draw bar. That's it!

If you find that the draw cone rotates when you tighten the nut, use a center punch and make a couple of dimples in the draw cone through the sawn slots. That will prevent the problem.

5. A relatively inexpensive band saw comes in handy to cut the slot freehand.

6. The finished mandrel is on the left. A stepped expansion mandrel that allows more show on the cap is on the right.

For smaller mandrels, instead of making a draw bar and cone, you can use a ¼-20 flathead bolt, 4½" long. The head has a taper angle of 82 degrees. You can get a countersink or combination center drill/countersink with that angle and use it to cut the internal taper to match the screw head. Note also that you can easily make advanced expansion mandrels like stepped mandrels that use two brass tubes. Such mandrels are not available commercially. They allow you to give a closed end pen more shape without the risk of hitting the brass tube edge (Photo 6).

Photo 7 shows a large clipless pen built with Ambassador parts, using the new cap mandrel.

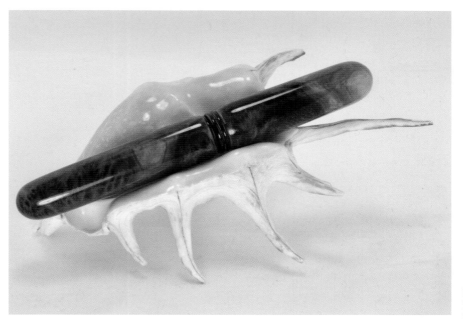

7. A large clipless, closed end pen, made using expansion mandrels.

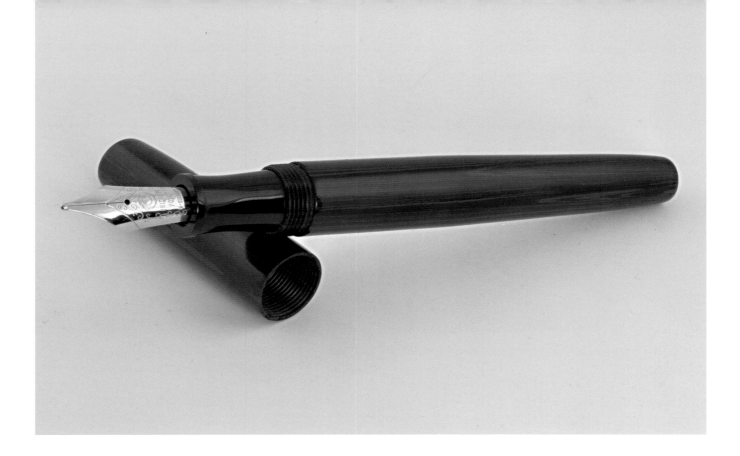

32. Clipless Fountain Pen from the Metal Lathe, Using Taps and Dies

To keep this pen simple we will use the El Grande grip and nib, which can be purchased without having to buy a complete kit. I will go through all of the steps. It is a great starting point for other designs. In this project we use commercially available taps and a die which is the easiest way to make threads. Actually this design can also be made on a wood lathe, as long as you have some sort of mandrel to hold the closed end barrels.

The tap for fitting the El Grande grip section is a metric M10 x 1.0. The El Grande cap uses a triple-lead thread, which means fewer turns to close. However, it is also a very expensive tap and die since they are custom-made. Instead, we use a ½" x 32 TPI tap and die for the cap. The male thread for the cap is right on top of the female thread for the nib section. This puts a limitation on the thread. ½" x 32 TPI can be found easily in the US, ½" x 28 TPI will also work very nicely and require less turns to close. You can even use ½" x 24 TPI and have enough material between the two threads that are on top of each other, or ¹⁵⁄₃₂" x 32 TPI. It is more difficult to obtain a good looking thread with a coarser tap and

Tools & Materials

- Lathe Metal lathe with standard accessories
- Die holder
- Tap prong
- Pen blank, acrylic acetate, resin, ebonite or similar
- ½" diameter minimum 12L14 steel rod (or drill rod)
- El Grande fountain pen grip and nib from Berea
- M10 x 1 metric tap and die
- ½" x 32TPI tap and die
- Drill bits "T", ⁵⁄₁₆", ¹⁵⁄₃₂", ⅜", ⁷⁄₁₆"

A. Main body

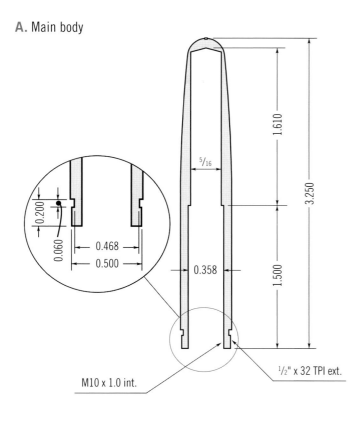

B. Cap

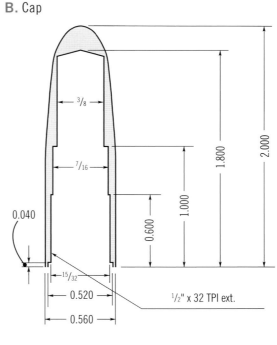

die. If you want to work metric, M12 x 0.8 is a good size. I will go over how to determine the proper bore sizes from the specific taps and dies so you can adapt to the tools you have.

The design is from the inside out, and restricted by the threading tools used. The thread for the grip section in the main body is dictated by the El Grande sections, M10 x 1.0. The drill size for a metric thread is the major diameter (first number, 10 mm) minus the pitch (1 mm, second number), i.e. 9 mm. 9 mm is 0.354". Letter "T" is 0.358 which is close enough. The upper section of the hole in the main body needs to accommodate the conversion pump or spare ink cartridge, ⁵⁄₁₆" gives enough clearance. The total length should be long enough to accommodate the conversion pump or two ink cartridges back to back. This measurement is taken off a grip section with pump inserted, and comes to 3.11".

The cap design is similar, from the inside out. The thread of ½" x 32 TPI dictates the bore. We can calculate the pitch by taking 1/TPI, therefore ⅓₂".

Again we subtract 1 pitch (⅓₂") from the major diameter ½" and arrive at ¹⁵⁄₃₂". So this is the hole we have to pre-drill for the thread. For the pen cap to thread on without cross threading, the front rim must not be able to move when the threads are ready to engage. This means the cap diameter has to be just a little more than the measurement we take off the front rim of the grip section, 0.430. So ⁷⁄₁₆" (.438") is a good size. The step has to occur 0.6" from the cap opening. Further up in the cap we can go even smaller, enough to clear the nib, ⅜" is enough. The transition from ⁷⁄₁₆" to ⅜" has to occur far enough back so the pen can close. Adding a little for safety gets us to 1". Drilling these steps allows more freedom with shaping the outside.

All the dimensions we will use are in Drawings A through D.

Start by turning the blank round, if it is square. I am using 16 mm cumberland (a hard rubber) here which is already round. Leave the diameter large at this point, at least ⅝". Cut a 2" piece for the cap and

C. The blueprint for the body mandrel.

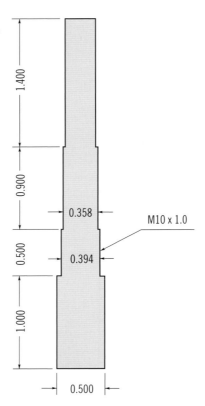

1.400

0.900

0.358

M10 x 1.0

0.500

0.394

1.000

0.500

D. The blueprint for the cap mandrel.

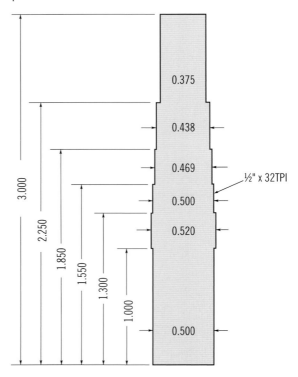

0.375

0.438

0.469

½" x 32TPI

0.500

0.520

3.000

2.250

1.850

1.550

1.300

1.000

0.500

3¼" for the body. We start with the body. Chuck the body blank in the lathe chuck or collet, leaving about 1" protruding. Face the end to have it square. Center drill the end, then drill to a depth of 1.5" with the "T" drill bit, using the drill chuck in the tail stock. It may be advantageous to drill with a slightly smaller diameter first, then clean up with "T" if the material has a tendency to melt. I am using cumberland (a hard rubber) for this pen which is fairly heat resistant. Follow this up with the ⁵⁄₁₆" drill bit, to a depth of 3.11". Again, you may want to do this in two stages. Many smaller lathes don't have a tailstock ram with that amount of travel, so mark the desired length off on the drill bit (Photo 1). Do not overdrill this hole because either a cartridge plus spare or a conversion pump must be held captive and not slip back out.

My grip section had a small recess, which the pen body needs to cover. You can use a boring bar or a HSS tool ground to an appropriate shape to cut a .385" recess to a depth of at least .040" (Photo 2). Alternatively you could turn a small trim ring out of stainless steel or aluminum to cover the step.

To tap on the lathe, the tap has to be held on axis. The simplest way to do this is with a tap guide, basically a spring-loaded point held in the tailstock chuck (Photo 3). You may need to experiment to find a good lubricant for the material you are cutting. Vegetable oil, either the spray kind like Pam or regular oil, applied with a small brush, turns out to be quite a good lubricant for many plastics. Apply some oil, and advance the tap, backing off ½ turn after every full turn. This breaks up the chips and avoids binding. Do not tap under power! To keep the chuck from turning, either put the lathe into the lowest gear, or

Tip: When drilling on the lathe, find out how far the tailstock ram travels for each revolution of the hand wheel. Many lathes use a 10 TPI leadscrew in the tailstock ram. So each revolution is ¹⁄₁₀". It's much easier to count revolutions than using the scale on the ram, and you can get ¼ turn (.025") accuracy easily.

1. Mark the drill depth on the drill bit using some tape.

2. A specially ground tool bit for machining small recesses.

3. Use a tap guide in the drill chuck to keep the tap straight, and use the chuck key to hold the chuck while tapping.

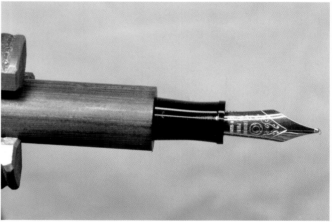

4. Test fit the grip section; there should be no gap.

use the chuck key to hold the chuck steady. Test the fit of the grip section to make sure there is no gap against the body (Photo 4).

Turn the body to a diameter of about .530" for a length of ¾". This will allow making the final pass when the body is reverse chucked. Turn a tenon with diameter 0.5" and a length of 0.2". The longer you make the tenon the more turns it will take to open/close the pen. If you end up with a longer tenon, you also have to make sure the nib still has room in the cap. Create an entry ramp for the die by putting a little chamfer on the edge using a file or lathe bit turned 45–60 degrees (Photo 5). Use the die in the die holder and again plenty of lubricant to cut the male thread for the cap, bringing the die right up against the step (Photo 6). Don't do this under power.

A tailstock die holder is essential. It is nearly impossible to cut a good thread on the lathe using a "die stock", a two-handled die holder, since you can't keep it square to the axis. Backing it up with something in the tailstock does not produce an accurate thread and it is very noticeable in the final pen. Add a small recess right next to the step for the threads to run out. The diameter should be the bore of the female cap thread, ¹⁵⁄₃₂" or .469" (Photo 7).

> *Tip:* Use a drinking straw with corrugated bend to blow out chips from closed-end barrels.

5. Create a small chamfer to allow the die to start and to prevent the end of the thread from breaking off.

6. Run the die right up to the step.

7. Create a runout groove for the thread using a specially ground narrow tool.

8. Test the cap on the body.

The cap is made in much the same way. Chuck up the blank; face the end and center drill. Drill the ⅜" hole to a depth of 1.8". Then widen the hole to ⁷⁄₁₆" for a depth of 1.0". Finally drill ¹⁵⁄₃₂" to a depth of 0.6". Use a boring bar or ground tool as shown in Photo 2 to create a small recess at the opening to let the cap overlap the pen a little. The pen body will be 0.520" so make the diameter .0522", a depth of around .030" is sufficient. Cut the cap thread using the ½" x 32 TPI tap with plenty of lubricant, with the tap guide in the tailstock. At this point you can test the fit with a grip section screwed into the body blank (Photo 8).

Now we have to make some custom mandrels. I use 12L14 steel since it machines like butter. You can also use drill rod or brass, if you have easy access to that. Brass will be a little more flexible, so you have to be extra careful with your cuts. Drawing C and Drawing

D show the dimensions. It is rather straightforward. Support the tailstock end using a live center after center drilling with a combination centerdrill/60 degree countersink. You can use the die holder to cut the M10 x 1.0 thread. The die will probably cut the .358" diameter section lightly, this is normal and does not interfere. Use plenty of cutting fluid! Photo 9 shows the two mandrels. You could also use custom expansion mandrels as shown in Chapter 31, but the threaded mandrels are more secure and accurate and do not have the potential for bulging out the barrel (which does not have a brass tube inside!).

Chuck the body mandrel up in an appropriate collet or chuck and thread on the pen body. The tailstock end is unsupported. Turn the pen body to .520" final diameter. There are several ways to give the body some shape. You can use woodworking chisels, or

9. Body and cap mandrel.

10. To allow the cap to post, create a taper on the body, using the as-yet unturned cap to test the fit.

set the compound to a slight taper followed by some work with a file to blend the shape, or just use a file. I like to transfer the mandrel to my wood lathe and shape using a gouge. Keep the internal bores in mind when you shape the body so you don't create a weak spot or break through! You can create a slight taper on the upper body to allow the cap to post (Photo 10). The cap should have a diameter of at least .560" at the thread because of the .522" recess we cut.

Finish with micro-mesh or your favorite plastic finishing technique. Wet micro-mesh lets me easily achieve a high sheen on cumberland.

The cap is made in exactly the same way. This pen does not have a clip. However, you could add one as shown in the next project.

The final pen is a real beauty! At 12 grams it is also very lightweight, lighter than any kit pen. I have found many people don't really care about a clip and will never put the pen in a shirt pocket. You can be creative and add some features that prevent the pen from rolling.

33. Custom Resin Fountain Pen

The last pen project uses a multi-start thread for the cap. Multi-start threads are convenient since it takes fewer turns to open and close a pen. You can also do this using taps and dies, but multi-start taps and dies in a size of interest are custom and very expensive. Once you learn to single-point cut a thread there are no such restrictions. Single-point thread cutting means cutting a spiral with the right pitch using a 60-degree point. You can grind your own bit, but I find it more convenient to use indexable tools, using a replaceable carbide bit. The tools I use for external and internal threads are shown in Photo 1. Each bit has three points. Once you get past the initial problems that typically involve a few crashes that leave you with a chipped bit, bits last for a long time, especially when just used on resins. The same carbide bits also cut threads in aluminum or steel. (You could actually cut the outside threads with the boring bar also, working behind the center.) You need a set of change gears that let you set up the proper pitch. Many more pitches than what is printed on the lathe or in the manual are possible by combining the gears in other ways. Thread-cutting theory is not for everyone, but there is lots of help available on the Internet. Note that you can cut very good metric threads on an imperial lathe and vice versa.

Tools & Materials

- Metal lathe with standard accessories
- Single-point exterior threading tool
- Single-point interior threading tool
- Resin rod, 16 mm or greater, 7.5" length, or 2 resin pen blanks
- ⅝" aluminum or stainless steel for center band
- Schmidt nib cartridge assembly from Richard Greenwald
- M6.4 x 0.5 tap from Richard Greenwald
- M10 x 1.0 mm tap and die
- Various drill bits
- Clip (from Baron kit)

A. A pen like this can't be made without plans.

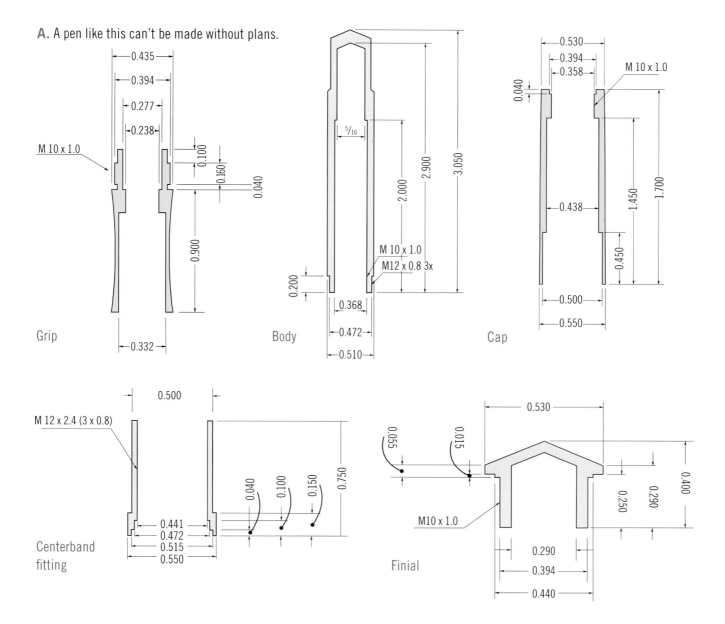

Grip

Body

Cap

Centerband fitting

Finial

I made a hand crank for the lathe spindle which is very handy. It is shown in Photo 2. It is much easier to thread using the crank than using lathe power. Often the lowest spindle speed is still fast, especially for a novice.

The blueprint for the pen is shown in Drawing A.

The design is from the inside out. We use an M10 x 1.0 thread for the section. The cap thread is M12 x .8 triple lead. This is the same size as used on the El Grande, but since we cut both threads we don't have to actually keep to that standard. For example, you could go a little larger to strengthen the center coupling a bit since an external thread is on top of an internal thread there. Or, if you want to avoid using

metric threads, you could use an appropriate imperial pitch.

The main body is designed just like the clipless pen. The grip section is made for the Schmidt nib cartridge. It uses an M6.4 x 0.5 thread, for which a tap is available from Richard Greenwald (see Resources on page 141). I like the Schmidt cartridge, since there is also a rollerball version available that can be screwed in. The rollerball will still use ink cartridges or the conversion pump. Externally I make the grip compatible with the El Grande section. The cap is made in two parts and uses a center band. I use a clip from a Baron kit on this pen. You can also adapt the design for some other clip that you might have.

B. Bushings are used to hold the grip section for shaping.

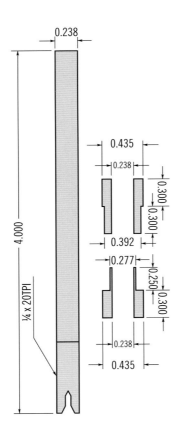

C. A mandrel to hold the center band fitting for machining the thin-walled tenon.

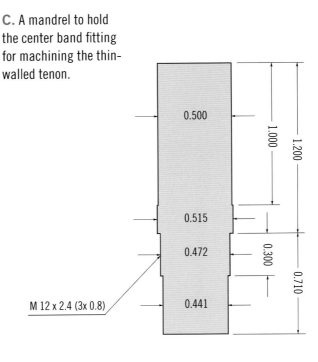

We start by making the grip section. The reason is that the nib carries the conversion pump, and the body has to clear the pump. Since I don't want to add extra length to deal with variations, it's best to start with this part. Cut a section 1.2" long and grab it in a collet. Face the end. Center drill and then drill through with a "B" (.238") or 6 mm drill. Then widen the hole to .332" for a depth of .720", using a "Q" drill bit. Tap the 6 mm section using an M6.4 x 0.5 tap and a tap guide to keep it straight (Photo 3). Vegetable oil makes a good lubricant, in cooking-spray form or applied with a brush. Go for about 10 full turns. Back up half a turn after every turn to keep the chips small and avoid binding when you back the tap out. Test the fit of the nib cartridge. Reverse the barrel in the collet, leaving about ½" protruding. Counterbore for the cartridge with a size "J" or 7 mm drill bit for a depth of .3". Turn the diameter down to .45". The reason for this will become obvious when we cut the section thread. Now turn a tenon with diameter .394" and a length of .35". This is for the section thread. Lastly, turn another tenon with diameter .335" and a length of .150". This is to clear the same thread and not bind in the main body which has a .358" bore.

Set up the lathe gears for a 1 mm pitch according to the gear chart for your lathe. On my 8x12 the

gearing is 80:68-60-72. See Photo 4. Mount the hand crank. Remember to never turn on the lathe power when the hand crank is mounted! Set the compound to an angle of 29.5-degrees where 0-degrees is perpendicular to the lathe axis, and parallel to the crossfeed. Set the compound dial to zero. Mount the threading tool and make sure it is exactly perpendicular to the lathe axis. A fishtail gauge is a handy device for that (Photo 5). Find the .394" surface with the tool by cranking the spindle and looking to *just* make contact, using the crossfeed only. At that point, set the crossfeed dial to read zero. Move the carriage to the right and engage the carriage on the lead screw. When cutting a metric thread on an imperial machine you can't make use of the threading dial. Once you engage the lead screw you need to stay engaged until the thread is completely cut. Advance the compound by .005" and crank the spindle until the tool nearly touches the .350" shoulder. This is the reason we turned the large diameter down to .350", to be able to cut closer to the shoulder. Withdraw the cross slide; don't touch the compound. Crank backward to go to the beginning of the thread, staying engaged to the lead screw. Bring the cross slide back to zero, and advance the compound by .003". Crank forward and the tool will follow the previous groove,

1. Threading tools. The interior tool can be used for exterior threads also, but working on the backside of the lathe.

2. A hand crank is very useful for threading, unless the lathe has extremely low gearing.

3. A tap guide is used to keep the tap straight on a lathe.

4. Change gears are used to set up the metric thread on the imperial lathe. The temporary piece of typing paper between the gears is a convenient way to set the proper clearance.

deepening it. Repeat this until the compound has advanced a total of .030", reducing the step size as you go. Keep lubricating with oil! It is possible that your specific bit has a different (tiny) flat spot in front, so perhaps the total feed is a little different. It pays to experiment on some scrap pieces first!

Why not use the M10 x 1.0 die to cut the male thread? Actually with the die there is much more force on the thin-walled workpiece, and I have sheared off the threads more than once.

Cut a groove .040" wide with a diameter of .344" at the end of the thread. Now you can remove the section from the spindle, remove the handle from the lathe, and disengage the lead screw. Make a short mandrel out of some size "B" drill rod and some bushings to hold the section (Drawing B). Turn the outer diameter to .430" and add a nice cove to the grip. You can do

that on a wood lathe or the metal lathe, using a file. Polish for a beautiful sheen (Photo 6)!

Cut a 3.05" long section from the stock you are using. Drill to a depth of 2" with a "T" bit. Follow this with the ⁵⁄₁₆" bit to a depth of 2.9". This 2.9" is taken from a measurement of the section with the nib in place and a conversion pump inserted. Since the section thread is a standard size, M10 x 1.0, I use a tap, with a tap guide to keep it straight. Don't forget to lubricate! It's important to cut this thread before the barrel is thinned, because it is very easy to crack a barrel instead of cutting a thread. Verify that the section with nib cartridge and conversion pump can be threaded on easily and fits well. Reduce the outside diameter to about .510" for a short length, to make room for the threading bit, then create a tenon with .472" diameter and .2" length.

5. A fishtail gauge is used to set the thread cutter square to the lathe. When there is no long, straight section of the workpiece available, sight against the lathe bed.

6. The finished grip section, all polished up.

7. The gearing for 2.4 mm (0.8 mm triple-lead) is not listed on the lathe but can be calculated. Information may also be found on the Internet.

8. The first groove of a triple-lead thread is cut.

Now we get to the cap thread. The pitch is .8", but we are using three entries for a steeper thread. This means there are three parallel grooves, and the actual pitch we need to set up for is 2.4 mm. This is a non-standard thread, and you will have to calculate the gearing. For the 8 x 12 you can find the gearing on the Internet, though some years ago I did the calculations and have my own table. The gearing on my 8 x 12 lathe is 72-30:68-80 (Photo 7). On my large Emco lathe, 2.4 mm pitch is also not labeled, but it is the same as a 10 TPI setting with the 127/120 metric gears in place. Other lathes like the popular 9 x 19 lathes have the same feature, the gear train is 40/60-127/120-30 with the feed-rate lever on the gear box in position four. (This is the 10 TPI pitch with the 127/120 reduction double added in).

The threads are cut one groove at a time. Again, it's a good idea to practice on some scrap first. As before, cut a groove, advancing the compound a total of .023" (Photo 8). For the next groove, we need to move the tool .08" to the left. Since we are coupled to the lead screw and must not let go until finished, this lateral motion involves the compound as well as the lead screw. Advance the compound by .063" from its zero starting position, and retract the cross-slide by .0545". Of course you need to retract further and approach the .0545" setting on an infeed motion because of backlash. Note that many lathes mark the cross-feed for diameter, each division on the dial being .002". This really means that for the actual motion, the cross slide moves .001" per division. The offset we need is .0545" direct motion, so 54½ divisions on the scale. The compound is generally

9. After moving the tool over exactly 1 pitch the second groove is cut.

10. The third groove completes the thread.

marked for direct motion, .001"/division. Carefully reset the dials to zero in those positions, without moving the tool. Cut the second groove, same as the first (Photo 9). Then repeat it all one more time for the third groove (Photo 10). Without disengaging the lead screw, move the carriage to the right to gain access to the thread. You can use an El Grande center band fitting to test the thread. If it is slightly tight, and the threads look even, under close inspection with a magnifier, you may have to make another pass going .001" deeper. Such variations are possible because of small differences between cutting tools. Again follow the offset between grooves (.063" on compound, -.0545" on cross slide) to deepen all 3 grooves. Make a note for next time that you need to go .024" instead of .023", or whatever your settings for your tool turn out to be.

The rest of the main barrel is straightforward. Use a mandrel as shown in Drawing B to hold the barrel while you turn, and sand and polish the outside. If you want to make the cap postable, you may want to hold off shaping the outside till the cap is finished.

The cap is made in four pieces. The threaded section is only ¾" long and is sleeved into the main body, making room for a center band. I make center bands out of 303 stainless steel. Aluminum or a contrasting resin or wood are also possibilities. The clip is held in place by a threaded finial. I use the clip from a Baron kit. Making the cap does not involve much that is new. Again there are some mandrels that need to be fabricated once. The internal threading uses a special tool, and a slightly different lathe setup. At first it may

feel odd to work on the inside of a barrel, not being able to see the cut, but it's the same sequence of operations as for the external thread.

We start by making the cap threads, the part that carries the center band (see Drawing A). Chuck up a ¾" long section of the material, having a diameter of ¾" or so. The length is chosen so that the grip section protrudes beyond it and keeps the pen aligned before the thread engages. This will prevent cross threading. Center drill with a ¹³⁄₃₂" drill. Use a boring bar to bring the internal diameter to .441". This is fairly critical. The starting drill, ¹³⁄₃₂" (.406"), is quite a bit undersize; it gives you room to sneak up on the diameter. Make a recess of .472" diameter for a depth of .100". This is to clear the uncut runout of the male thread. Then cut a second recess with diameter .515" to allow a slight overlap of the cap over the main body. Set up the compound to -29.5-degrees (to the left) (Photo 11). Mount the threading tool and see whether there is clearance to cut the thread to a depth of .4". If you cannot move the tool there, you need to swing the tool rest 180-degrees from that position, to the back. Find the .472" surface and set cross feed and compound dials to zero. The internal thread is cut with the same sequence of operations as the external thread. The total amount of feed with the compound is .021". If the fit is too tight, you may have to use .022". It depends on the tool radius at the cutting tip of your specific tool. After the 1st groove is cut, move the compound .063" towards the front (operator side), and the cross slide towards the back by .0545". After all three grooves are cut, move the carriage to

11. The interior threading tool ready for use. Notice the compound is swung 29.5 degrees to the left for the proper feed.

12. A test fit verifies a good thread. The carriage should remain engaged to the lead screw.

13. The center band fitting on a short shopmade mandrel.

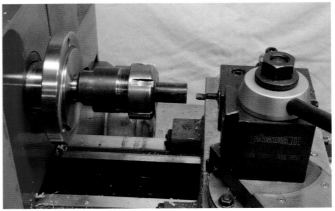

14. A boring bar is used to cut a recess for the center band fitting.

the right without disengaging the lead screw and try the body (Photo 12).

Reverse-mount the insert on a mandrel as per Drawing C. This mandrel, being very short, can be made from aluminum or brass. I use 12L14 steel for mine. Turn the outer diameter to .550". Round over the left edge with a small file or some sandpaper, and polish with micro-mesh. Then turn the sleeved part to a diameter of .500" for a length of .600" (Photo 13). You can turn a center band to fit onto that .5" sleeve, the design has it as .150" in length. Make the cross-sectional thickness .025" for the ring to sit flush.

Next is the cap body. It is fairly straightforward. Chuck up a 1.7" long piece of the resin rod, center drill and drill with $^{7}/_{16}$" to a depth of 1.45". This leaves .25" for the finial thread. Drill through the rest of the way using a "T" drill bit, the proper tap drill for the

M10 x 1.0 thread used for the finial. Use a boring bar to open up the cap to a diameter of .500" and a depth of .450" for the insert (Photo 14). Make sure the insert with the center band slipped on fits. There should be no gap inside at the end of the sleeve or outside at the center band. Reverse the cap and tap with M10 x 1.0 using a tap and tap guide. Mount the cap on a mandrel using shop-made bushings (Drawing D). I made a screw-in bushing for the upper end. Shape the cap outside, using a file and sand paper, using any combination of turning, filing and sanding. Sand and polish with micro-mesh.

The last item to make is the finial. You have to make sure there is adequate room for the nib inside the finial, so put the cap on the pen and check where the tip of the nib ends up with respect to the end of the cap. In this case it protrudes about .050", so this has to be taken into account for making the finial.

D. Bushings to hold the cap for exterior shaping.

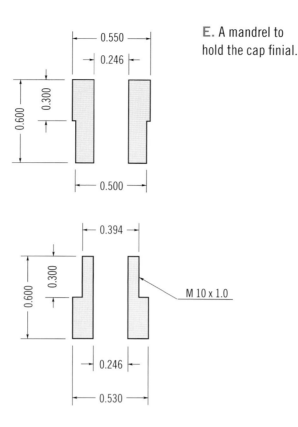

0.550
0.246
0.300
0.600
0.500

0.394
0.300
0.600
M 10 x 1.0
0.246
0.530

E. A mandrel to hold the cap finial.

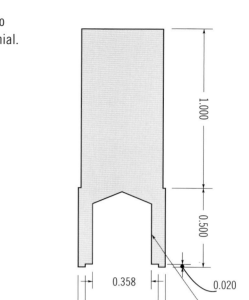

1.000
0.500
0.358
0.445
0.020
0.530
M 10 x 1.0

The blueprint Drawing A shows .055" in accordance with this measurement but it's easy to be off a little so a measurement and appropriate adjustment are in order. By now all the machining operations are routine. Chuck up a resin rod, turn the diameter to .530". Turn a tenon .25" long and .394" in diameter. Single-point cut a M10 x 1.0 thread, or use a die. Drill out a cavity to make room for the tip of the nib with an "L" (.290") drill for a depth of 0.29" measured at the drill shoulder. Cut a step .440" in diameter for .015", a little less than the thickness of the clip ring. This will center and clamp the clip ring. Part off the finial, reverse-mount it in a mandrel that is tapped M10 x 1.0 (drawing E), and shape and polish the outside.

Epoxy the threaded insert into the cap body. If you have not shaped the body, now is the time to do that and provide a taper for the cap to fit on. The details are your preference. Assemble clip and finial on the cap, and sit back and admire your beautiful custom pen!

This project serves as a general introduction to many of the basic techniques used in making a pen on a metal lathe. Building on this you can take a look at a classic pen and make a similar pen in the material of your choice. It's beyond the scope of this introduction to get into details like the fill mechanism, decorations, and such. You are limited only by your imagination and the willingness to try things. A lot can be done on the lathe! A small metal lathe with some basic tooling opens the horizon of what you can do; and the investment is not that large. I used a lathe I bought for less than $500 for all these projects: a lathe that at the time of this writing is still one of the incredible bargains out there and with more capability than I can use.

Section VII:
Frequently Asked Questions, Problems, Shortcuts and Tricks

How to avoid and deal with drilling blowouts

Drilling pen blanks is discussed in detail in Chapter 2. The best way to prevent drilling blowouts, as shown in Photo 1 is to cut the blank long, do not let the drill bit exit, then cut the barrel to length. The barrel shown in the picture can actually be repaired as long as the gap can be closed completely by pushing the pieces back together using clamps. Flow a thin line of CA along the seam; it will wick in. If you add glue first, then try to close the gap, the seam is usually more visible. Under a CA finish such a repair will often be completely invisible, even to the pen maker.

Another cause for blowouts is chips that are not clearing out of the hole during drilling, but instead are getting packed into the drill flutes (Photo 2). Certain woods are very prone to this. For example, oily, dense, woods such as cocobolo, African blackwood or desert ironwood. When you begin drilling, chips clear out of the hole easily, but as you drill deeper, the chips may stop getting transported up the flutes and exiting. Once the flutes become clogged and you continue drilling, the removed material has no place to go. You create a lot of heat as well as pressure in the hole. This can lead to cracking as you get towards the bottom. To prevent this from happening, withdraw the drill bit all the way and clear the packed chips. Continue drilling a little at a time, retract and clear frequently.

A cracked or blown out partially drilled barrel is not necessarily a loss. You can use thin or medium CA and a clamp to repair the crack, then carefully re-drill the hole. If the gap closes uniformly, you may never see the crack line.

Dealing with blowouts while turning

Blowouts during turning are usually due to a catch. Catches are a fact of life; with better cutting techniques you will get fewer over time, but I don't think you'll find a turner that never gets a catch. Some unexpected grain, a moment of inattention is all it takes. Occasionally, if you keep an exceptionally clean area around your lathe, you may be able to find the piece and glue it back on with medium CA.

1. Drilling blow-outs frequently happen when the bit exits the blank.

2. Keep an eye on the chips. When they start packing into the flutes heat and pressure can crack blanks.

A small area in the middle of a blank can sometimes be filled with wood shavings or dust and CA. Pack the hole with shavings. Wick some thin CA into them, followed by a drop or two of medium CA. Give it a minute to dry, hit it with accelerator, and continue turning. The repair may become invisible, especially in a burl. Note that if you use sawdust it will get darker when you add CA which in a burl

3. This little critter once was a accidental hole. Enlarged and filled with crushed stone it adds something unique to the pen.

6. You would never know that the accent started out as a problem.

4. Turn a tenon to remove a problem near the end of a barrel.

5. The repair used a cutoff from the same piece of wood and it looks like it belongs there.

may disappear, but on straight grained wood may not work well. You can also use crushed stone to fill a hole. For a contrasting fill, you can mix epoxy with some sawdust and work it into the hole with a toothpick. Treat a hole as a design opportunity, enlarge it with a Dremel tool or similar before you fill it (Photo 3).

A blowout near the end of a barrel can also be filled with epoxy and sawdust. Overfill the area, and once the epoxy has cured, re-square the barrel (using sandpaper rather than a pen mill) and continue turning.

Another repair method is to remove the defective area while the barrel is on the lathe (Photo 4) and add a new section made from matching wood. A cutoff from the same pen blank comes in handy! Hide the junction either by adding a thin contrasting piece of wood or another contrasting material (Photo 5). You can also just butt the new wood against the old piece, then make a groove at the junction. The groove should go nearly all the way down to the brass tube. The groove is then filled with crushed stone. To add crushed stone, make a small stone heap in the groove, and wick in a drop of thin CA using a micro-nozzle. Use just enough to hold the stone in place. Be careful not to use too much CA so it runs into the bottom of the groove! Now rotate the blank a bit, make another little stone heap, the first one will help keep it in place, and again wick in CA. Work your way around the blank. I find a carbide-tipped tool useful for turning the stone down to the wood level. Recess the stone slightly below the surface. Then add some CA to bring it back up. Photo 6 shows a finished repaired pen. We refer to such a decorative accent often as an oops-band; but only you will know that it was not a planned accent.

7. With a bent mandrel you can still turn a round barrel but the eccentricity will render this barrel unusable.

"Non-round" pens

Most turned pen barrels are round. It's the nature of a lathe to make round things! So, why when a pen is assembled sometimes do the barrels appear out-of-round? In most cases, the barrels are still round, but are eccentric (Photo 7). Which means the turned wood is not on the same axis as the brass tube, and where the wood meets the fitting one side is high. Frequently this means the mandrel, during turning, was not straight. First, check the mandrel as outlined in Chapter 7. Then make sure the blanks are squared properly to the axis. Use a pen mill and well-fitting shim barrel or an accurate sanding jig as shown in the Chapter 4 sidebar *Making an Accurate Squaring Jig for your Belt or Disk Sander* (page 23). If the end faces are not square, this can add a bend to the mandrel when the mandrel nut is tightened. Lastly, make sure the mandrel nut is not too tight. During roughing, the mandrel nut can self-tighten. So it is a good practice to rough the barrels, and once they are round, stop the lathe, loosen the mandrel nut and re-tighten it just enough to keep the barrel from turning. At the same time, any pressure on the mandrel from the tailstock live center should also be relaxed. The live center should just support the mandrel, not put pressure on it. Of course, lathe chisels should be sharp.

The other possibility is that the barrel truly is not round. That can happen if you used too much sandpaper. Wood is not uniform; the growth rings have different degrees of hardness. When you sand excessively to get the barrel to the final dimension, the softer earlywood area can sand away faster than the harder latewood areas. To avoid this, do all the shaping with your chisels, and minimize sanding. It can be helpful to soak the wood with thin CA to make it more uniform in hardness. This is especially useful when dealing with very soft, punky material found in spalted woods that were not stabilized.

Avoiding splits during assembly

Splits during assembly are the result of two conditions. Frequently some dried glue left inside the brass tube is to blame. Avoid getting glue inside the barrel by plugging the end of the brass tube that is inserted into the blank, using Play-Doh or dental wax. A slice of potato or apple can also be used. Use the brass tube like a cookie cutter. Despite such precautions you can still get some glue inside. Use a hobby knife, a small pocketknife, a gun barrel brush, a proper size drill bit, or a round file. For 7 mm brass tubes, a chainsaw file is also a good size.

The other reason that a barrel can split during assembly is that parts are not staying aligned. An assembly press that keeps parts aligned is helpful. Also, make sure there is no burr on the brass tube. Use a deburring tool as shown in the photo on page 26. On a simple arbor press, start the fitting in the barrel by hand, make sure it is straight, then keep it squarely on the base while you press it home.

For critical materials like ivory where you want to avoid any risk during assembly, file out the brass tube until the fitting slides in freely, then epoxy it in place.

Cracking after assembly

This is usually due to retained moisture in the wood. As wood dries on a brass tube it shrinks, but the brass tube prevents it from moving so it cracks. Avoid problems by using kiln dried or stabilized woods. There are some woods that are notorious for cracking. Review Chapter 10 for some techniques that help minimize the danger.

Ballpoint writing tip extension issues

A ballpoint tip should have sufficient extension, and retract fully. The proper extension is shown in Photo 8. Note how the slope of the refill is an extension of the slop of the tip, when the refill is fully extended. Too short an extension makes the pen uncomfortable to write with, because you have to hold it at a rather steep angle. If the tip does not retract fully, it may soil shirt pockets or pocketbook contents. On a 7 mm pen, the amount of tip extension is fully adjustable via the transmission: If it does not extend enough, remove the refill and use a press to push the transmission in a little more.

If the refill on a 7 mm pen extends too far, disassemble the pen (tip and transmission), re-insert the tip, and then press in the transmission the proper amount. Use the 3 ¹⁵⁄₁₆" gauge shown in the photo on page 57. An alternative method was shown to me many years ago by my friend Jim Lane. Take a 2" piece of pen blank, drill a ⅛" hole in it, and then rip it down the middle on a band saw. Slide a 7 mm bushing followed by a washer over the transmission and grip it in the two soft jaws you just made, in a vise. Use two screwdrivers as a lever to push the pen body up slightly until the refill extension is right (Photo 9).

For Parker-style refills, the transmission usually screws into a fitting that is not adjustable. In many cases it is pressed into the front barrel. If it does not extend far enough, you can disassemble the pen and shorten the body slightly using a sander with squaring jig. Do this at the pen center, so you don't affect the critical fit of the tip. You can also use a belt sander to shorten the transmission near the front so

it seats a little lower. Make sure the end stays square. Remove all of the brass dust using a Q-tip, or by pushing a piece of paper towel into the transmission. The towel can then be removed with a tweezers.

8. Proper ballpoint tip extension.

9. You can correct a tip that does not retract enough on a 7 mm pen without major disassembly.

10. A quick fix for a refill that does not retract on a Parker pen. For in-house use only.

11. Turn a dowel to fit inside a brass tube. Proceed to part off a narrow ring.

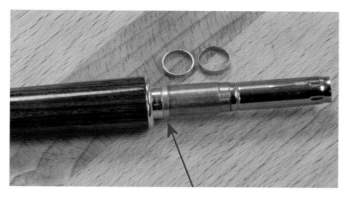

12. A small brass spacer moves the transmission up a little to let a Parker-style refill tip retract fully.

If the tip of a Parker refill does not retract fully, you can do a quick and dirty fix by grinding a little off the plastic end of the refill (Photo 10). For a pen that leaves your immediate family this is obviously not a good enough solution. On a cigar pen, you can turn a replacement ring that goes between the very tip and the tip adapter. It's a little tricky to get length and two diameters just right. Another option is to turn a small spacer from a piece of plastic, aluminum or a spare brass tube and slip it onto the transmission fitting before the transmission is added. To turn a spacer from a brass tube, first turn a dowel that fits inside the brass tube (Photo 11). This lets you part off a narrow ring which you can then fix in place with a little epoxy. (Photo 12). It is also possible to lengthen a barrel, by letting a barrel extension extend beyond the end of the brass tube. Photos 13 through 17 shows such a repair. One additional issue you might run into occasionally is that the hole in the pen tip is too tight or deformed and the refill might be stuck. You can test this by inserting the refill from the front. The tip should slide freely through the hole. If it does not, use a #38 drill bit (.101") and ream out the tip.

13. A cigar pen refill that does not retract enough.

14. Expose the brass tube.

15. Add some of the same wood, beyond the brass tube end. Use the brass tube from another kit as a gauge to set the proper length.

16. The new, longer tube, with wood extending beyond the brass tube.

17. The finished repair. The junction to the new wood was hidden with a wire-burned decoration.

Hiding brass tubes in acrylic pens

To avoid seeing brass tubes through acrylic pens, paint the inside of the drilled hole with a matching paint. See Chapter 8 for a discussion of techniques.

Disassembling pens

For 7 mm pens you can buy a disassembly kit with good instructions at any kit supplier.

Many other pens can be disassembled by knocking out fittings with appropriately sized rods. A set of transfer punches makes a great universal disassembly kit that will probably cover 95% of your needs. Discount tool suppliers have inexpensive sets in ¹⁄₆₄" increments. They are also available from Penn States Industries. Place the pen barrel in your hand, insert the knockout rod and hit it a few times with a

18. A commercial knock-out plug next to a homemade one.

19. A homemade slide hammer allows disassembly of closed end barrels. Add adapters as needed for other pens.

hammer. A piece of router mat increases the diameter of the barrel and provides a better non-slip grip.

When the access holes on both sides are the same size this method does not work. Craft Supplies USA supplies a screw-in plug with some of their kits (e.g. the Junior Statesman) that can be screwed into one fitting and allows knocking out the plug and fitting as one unit. With a metal lathe you can make similar plugs for other kits. Photo 18 shows a Junior Statesman plug next to one I made for Berea's El Grande.

Closed end pens provide a special challenge. There are no commercial solutions for disassembly that I am aware of. I made a slide hammer for this type of pen (Photo 19), and with a series of specialized adapters, I am able to disassemble closed end pens also. To use, screw the rod into the fitting, then slide the weight repeatedly against the washer on the other end.

Click pens are often difficult to disassemble. You often end up breaking little plastic parts. Time to call the supplier for a replacement mechanism!

Hard-to-twist ballpoint pens

Transmissions can be hard to twist as you get them from the supplier. When you have a twist pen that is difficult to operate, first remove the transmission and check that by itself it operates freely. On a 7 mm pen, remove the refill and see that it operates easily. On an 8 mm pen usually the lower part of the transmission has to turn within the upper pen barrel. So before assembling the pen, make sure that the lower part

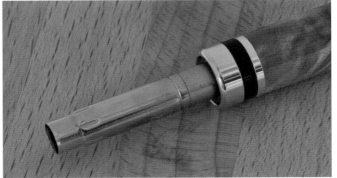

20. Before assembling 8 mm pens reverse the transmission and test the fit in the barrel. It has to slide freely.

has enough clearance within the upper barrel (Photo 20). If there is glue inside the upper barrel, clear it out with a small knife. On some pens, you press a center band directly onto an exposed brass tube tenon. This can collapse the brass tube sufficiently for the transmission to hang up. Use a letter "L" drill bit to ream out the brass tube if necessary. Another area to check is if the center band itself is rubbing on a slightly fat, lower barrel. This can be checked by removing the transmission and refill and carefully inspecting that area for contact. If it hangs up there, the best thing to do is disassemble the lower barrel and reshape to provide clearance.

What is the best finish to use?

Unfortunately there is no universal answer to this question. For resins, it's straightforward. Sand, then polish and buff with one or several of a myriad of compounds till you get the finish you are happy with. Wet or dry may be dictated by the availability of water near your lathe. For wood, the choices are numerous. Not everyone likes the same finish. Some people prefer a matte finish, others (myself included) a high gloss. Balancing effort against results is where it's at. Lacquer makes a good finish that will hold up well. You need to apply several coats. To me, CA glue provides the best finish. Once you have applied a sufficiently thick layer, it's like polishing another plastic. I am happy with the finish I can achieve in a relatively short time; until I see my pens next to someone else's that look better! Then it's time to experiment again. The key to a good finish is practice. This sounds trivial, but is especially true here.

If your CA finish has dull spots, you've polished through the finish. The best way to recover is to apply another layer or two and start over.

Small defects can sometimes be hidden under the clip.

What is the best drill bit to use?

The best drill bit is a sharp drill bit. This really is the most important thing. Twist drills, kept sharp with a Drill Doctor or similar jig and ground to a split point work well, especially if you provide an entry point by dimpling the wood with a center punch. I am partial to pilot-point drill bits, they drill very straight but they are hard to sharpen.

Who makes the best pen kits?

All pen kits are made in Taiwan or, as of lately, China. At the time of this writing the Chinese-made kits seem to be of a little lower quality, but I would expect this to change with time. The main importers all tend to stand behind their products.

Removing glue from fingers

Avoidance goes a long way, but I don't really like working with gloves. I use a porous stone with soap and water to remove dried glue. The product is called Glue-B-Gone and is available in hobby stores. It even does an admirable job with polyurethane glue.

Interchanging bushings and mandrels

There are two sizes of mandrels, the so-called 7 mm mandrel or size "A" and the 8 mm mandrel or size "B". Bushings do not interchange between the systems! For some kits, you have a choice of "A" or "B" size bushings from different suppliers. To a limited degree it is possible to mix bushings and mandrels from different manufacturers, but fit is not guaranteed. In some cases you end up with bushings that are loose on a mandrel, thus introducing an additional error. You can also get bushings that are too tight to fit on a mandrel. These could be carefully reamed out or opened up with a small round file. It's best to keep bushings and mandrels within a supplier.

The following pages show examples of work by some of the top pen makers in the country. These pieces are examples of where you can take the basic techniques I have shown in this book.

Section VIII: Gallery

Jeff Powell

ABOVE: *Soaring Eagle*
This rollerball style pen is hand crafted from aluminum and brass rods and shotgun shell parts. The pen body is resin cast by Jeff and the clip is hand cut and heat bent sheet brass.

ABOVE RIGHT: *Rain Dance*
Inspired by the rainy season, this is a custom ballpoint pen with aluminum parts and an acrylic body. Each rain drop is hand cut with a scroll saw. The pattern revolves completely around the pen ending with a splash into the nib.

RIGHT: *Skull and Bones*
One of his most popular pen designs, this includes a hand cut and inlaid acrylic skull and cross bones along with custom turned aluminum parts. This is a ballpoint Parker style pen. The button on top turns to activate the refill.

Barry Gross

RIGHT: Coins were recovered from the shipwrecked Le Chameau which sunk in 1725. The coins were bent by hand around the painted pen tubes and then coated with clear acrylic. An 18kt gold nib is added to this classy fountain pen.

BELOW: Many different watches were dis-assembled and the gears and springs are bent to fit the diameter of the pen tube. The pen tubes are then coated in acrylic, turned and polished to the high gloss finish. Barry calls this his 'recycled series'.

Mark Gisi

LEFT: Wood, turquoise Tru-stone, sterling silver and more materials are exquisitely combined with hammered copper parts to create this custom rollerball pen. Mark has taken the art of segmented pens to new heights.

RIGHT: A stained glass inspired pen featuring a combination of several woods and acrylics to create a pattern based upon chevrons.

Dan Symonds

RIGHT: Modern safety style pen in an acrylic tortoise shell body with a synthetic ivory overlay in a floral motif. The nib fully retracts into the body by twisting the finial.

BELOW: Green, hard rubber with an Italian acrylic overlay in a Celtic knot motif.

Michael Roux

Aluminum ballpoint pen with windows opening up a view to a braided sleeve center.

Pat Lawson

BELOW: Pat used millifiore clay applied on brass tubes then fired and turned very thin, and finally cast in clear acrylic for this rollerball pen.

BELOW RIGHT: A ballpoint pen, millifiore clay cast in clear acrylic.

Kurt Hertzog

FAR LEFT: Dip pen done in cherry with black gesso. Painted with acrylic paint, and finished with a spray lacquer. Shown on a desk stand of white Corian with turned blackwood pegs.

LEFT: Using long brass tubes, and a segmented design made from walnut, yellowheart, and maple this is another variation on a 7 mm kit pen without the center band. Shown in a delicate desk stand of turned and pierced cherry.

Don Ward

RIGHT: Postage stamps were scanned and printed with an inkjet printer on self-adhesive labels that were then wrapped on a brass tube and cast in clear acrylic.

FAR RIGHT: Don cast prairie rattlesnake in a clear acrylic and added walnut ends to the upper barrel of this custom 7 mm ballpoint pen.

Brian Gisi

RIGHT: A large fountain pen done in a medieval motif. The pen is turned from a combination of ebonite, African blackwood, afzalia burl and buckeye burl. The pen features sterling silver accents and a segmented "stone" design with individual pieces of buckeye burl separated by an acetate "mortar."

LEFT: A mid-sized roller ball done in an industrialized art deco motif. The pen is turned from hard rubber and celluloid and features sterling silver accents and a machined aluminum nose cone. Brian designs and casts his own sterling silver parts.

Steven Jackson

BELOW: Steel Rods ballpoint and fountain pen. Made with stainless steel welding rods. (Photo: Steven Jackson)

ABOVE: Bullet Casing ballpoint pen, made with copperhead snake skin and Winchester 308 bullet casings. Stainless steel trim. (Photo: Steven Jackson)

Resources

Woodcraft
pen kits, tools, materials
mailorder and many retail stores
http://www.woodcraft.com/
1-800-225-1153

Rockler Woodworking and Hardware
pen kits, tools, materials
mailorder and many retail stores
http://www.rockler.com/
1-800-279-4441

Lee Valley Tools Ltd.
pen kits, tools, materials
mailorder and retail stores (Canada)
http://leevalley.com/
1-800-871-8158

Berea Hardwoods Co., Inc.
pen kits, tools, materials
mailorder and retail store
http:/penkits.com/
1-877-736-5487

Craft Supplies USA
pen kits, tools, materials
mailorder and retail store
http://woodturnerscatalog.com/
1-800-551-8876

Penn State Industries
pen kits, tools, materials
mailorder and retail store
http://www.pennstateind.com/
1-800-377-7297

Arizona Silhouette, Inc.
pen kits, tools, materials
online, mailorder
http://www.arizonasilhouette.com/
1-928-329-9466

Beartooth Woods
pen kits, tools, materials
online, mailorder
http://www.beartoothwoods.com
1-719 532 1756

Woodturningz Inc.
pen kits, tools, materials
online, mailorder
http://woodturnignz.com
1-888-736-5487

Packard Woodworks, Inc.
pen kits, tools, materials
online, mailorder
http://www.packardwoodworks.com/
1-800-683-8876

The Beall Tool Company
tools, spiralling jig
online, mailorder
http://www.bealltool.com/
1-800-331-4718

Klingspor's Woodworking Shop
sanding supplies, tools
online, mailorder, stores
http://woodworkingshop.com/
1-800-228-0000

Richard Greenwald, LLC
pen parts
online, mailorder
http://www.richardlgreenwald.com/
11501 Front Field Lane
Potomac, Maryland 20854

Beta Diamond Products
diamond polishing paste
online, mailorder
http://www.betadiamond.com/
1-800-975-9009

Elen Hunting and Importing
deer antler, tusk ivory
online, mailorder
http://www.elenhunting.com/
1-800-319-9145

The Perfect Collection
mandrels for Pentel pencils
online, mailorder
http://www.theperfectcollection.com/

BG Artforms
pen kits, polishing supplies
online, mailorder
http://bgartforms.com/
1-888-717-4202

Kallenshaan Woods
laser-cut pen kits
online. mailorder
http://kallenshaanwoods.com

Classic Nib
pen kits, fountain pen nibs, tools
online, mailorder
http://www.classicnib.com/

Enco
metal lathes and tools
online, mailorder
http://www.use-enco.com
1-800-873-3626

MSC Industrial Supply Co.
tools, hardware
online, mailorder
http://www.mscdirect.com/
1-800-645-7270

McMaster-Carr
tools, hardware
online, mailorder
http://www.mcmaster.com/
1-609-689-3415

Grizzly Industrial, Inc
tools, pen kits, materials
online, mailorder, show rooms
http://www.grizzly.com/
1-800-523-4777

Harbor Freight
metal lathes and tools
online, mailorder, retail stores
http://www.harborfreight.com/
1-800-444-3353

Exotic Blanks
specialty pen blanks
online, mailorder
http://www.exoticblanks.com/
1867 Taylor Ave
Racine, WI 53403

Boone Trading Company
mammoth ivory, tusks, horn
online, mailorder
http://boonetrading.com/
1-800-423-1945

Penturners Group on yahoo!
internet forum and online resource
http://groups.yahoo.com/group/
penturners/

Then Penmakers' Guild
internet forum and online resource
http://groups.yahoo.com/group/
PenMakersGuild/

IAP
internet forum and online resource
http://www.penturners.org

The Penshop
internet forum and online resource
http://www.thepenshop.net

Index

A

Abralon 42-44
accelerator 53, 69, 81
acrylic acetate 39, 98, 114
acrylic paint 40, 99
acrylic pen blank 58, 98
acrylics 41
aerosol accelerator 31
African blackwood 62, 65, 91, 129, 140
afzalia burl 140
airline drill 111, 112
almond wood 91
aluminum 26, 55, 56
aluminum oxide wheels 4
Ambassador cap 111
Ambassador parts 113
angle cut woods 38
antler 11, 16, 44
antler cigar pen 42
antler drilling 12
anvil 26, 27
"A" precision mandrel 5
arbor press 27, 131
arizonasilhouette.com 29, 30, 70, 101, 111
Art Deco 18
Artist's Sketch Pencil kit 81
assembly gauge 66
assembly press 57
axis deer 42

B

ball-end cutters 102
ballpoint tip 132
band saw 4, 15, 19, 20, 29, 34, 40, 42, 46, 50, 55, 58, 59, 60, 76, 79, 81, 83, 85, 112, 113, 132
Baron fittings 31
Baron kit 120, 121, 125
Baron pen 29
barrel trimmer 6, 22, 34, 43, 54, 61
bastard file 20

Beall chuck 76
Beall collet chuck 5, 43, 48
Beall, JR 88
Beall Master Turner 87
Beall Pen Wizard 88, 95
Beall Tool Co. 87, 90
belt sander 22, 23, 43, 46, 61, 74, 76, 82, 85, 132
belt setting 3
bench vises 26
Berea 5, 39, 40, 55, 57, 93, 114
Berea Hardwoods 18, 41, 71, 101
Berea's El Grande 134
Bethlehem olive wood 70, 71
bevel rubbing 30
birdseye maple 14, 67
Black and Decker 9
black ash burl 48
blackwood 139
block plane 13
bloodwood 80, 83, 90, 91
blowouts 13, 29, 129, 130
boring bar 112
bowl gouge 3
"B" precision mandrel 5
bradpoint bit 8
brick pattern pen 81
buckeye burl 140
'bullet bit' 9
burl 14, 29, 30, 67, 129
busy-block 16

C

CA (cyanoacrylate) glue 3, 21, 29, 31, 37, 41, 43, 44, 46, 51, 52, 53, 54, 61, 63, 64, 65, 68, 69, 74, 79, 80, 81, 82, 83, 85, 91, 95, 96, 109, 129-131, 135
calipers 31, 38, 46, 61, 64, 73, 76, 106, 111
carbide bit 120
carnauba wax 92-94, 103
carpenter's glue 79, 81
centering drill 9, 111
center prong 5
center spur 8

chamfer 108, 117, 118
cherry 139
Chilean lapis 33
China 135
chop saw 19, 58, 84
cigar pen 43, 133
clamps 26
Classic Nib 11
Click Polaris 100
clipless fountain pen 114
clip recess 51
closed-end barrels 117
closed end mandrels 111
closed end pens 70, 74, 113, 134
cloth-backed sandpaper 25
cocobolo 10, 12, 129
collet chuck 36, 44, 50, 62, 64, 66, 68-70, 73-75, 95, 106, 116, 118, 122
collet holders 107
'Comfort' 57
conversion pump 71, 115, 116, 122, 123
Corian 15, 18, 22, 26, 49, 66, 139
Cove-Spiral Pen 101
Craft Supplies USA 18, 26, 29, 33, 45, 57, 62, 99, 134
Cross-style refill 58
crushed stone 95, 96, 130
crushed turquoise 62, 64, 95, 97
CSU 81, 83
cumberland 115, 116, 119
curly maple 14
Custom Resin Fountain Pen 120
cutter bit 101
cutting fluid 106, 118
cutting oil 111, 112
cutting spur 8

D

DC motors 3
Delrin 56, 109
Delrin sleeve 35
Deming 9
depth stop 7, 8
desert ironwood 12, 80, 91, 129
desk pen 67, 69, 74

'detail gouge' 3
DeWalt 9
die holder 106, 108, 111, 114, 117, 118
disassembly kit 134
disk sander 21, 22, 24, 49, 52, 54, 82, 85
draw cone 112
Dremel 4, 63, 65, 90, 95, 98, 101, 130
drill axis 13, 84
drill bit 2, 7-13, 18, 20, 22, 29, 33, 34, 39, 40, 42-44, 46, 48-50, 55, 59, 65, 67, 68, 70, 72, 74, 76, 81, 95, 98, 101, 102, 109, 110, 112, 116, 117, 120, 122, 126, 129, 131, 133, 135
drill chart 13
drill chuck 7-9, 11, 20, 62, 66, 67, 105-107, 116, 117
Drill Doctor 9, 135
drill guide 7
drilling blanks 11
drill jig 7, 10, 11, 12
drill path 11
drill press 7, 8, 10-12, 26
drill press quill 8
drill vise 44
dymondwood 14, 38

E

E6000 adhesive 46
eBay 9, 15, 41, 44
ebonite 114, 140
ebony 19, 80, 83
EEE Ultrashine 25, 26
Electra 101
Electra brass tube 96
Electra kit 95
Elegant Sierra 18
elephant ivory 45
El Grande 77, 109, 115, 121, 125
El Grande cap barrel 55
El Grande grip 114
El Presidente brass tube 70
El Presidente kit 71